Baidu

An in-depth exploration of the political economy of the Chinese technology company Baidu which, along with China's other tech giants Alibaba and Tencent, has emerged as a leading global Internet company.

Baidu – not Google – is the dominant search company in China, the largest Internet market in the world, whose impact on the political economy is no longer limited to China, but the broader global market, and in particular the US economy. This book outlines the intense competition within the search engine market and illustrates the inter-capitalist dynamic in the contemporary Chinese Internet sector, and highlights Baidu's uniqueness on the global stage as it pivots to Artificial Intelligence (AI) and expands into other industrial sectors. ShinJoung Yeo offers a window into the intensifying geopolitical shaping of the global Internet industry, and the contention and collaboration among multinational firms and states to control the most dynamic capitalist economic sector – the Internet.

An important and timely analysis for anyone interested in the political economy of the global media, communication, and information industries, and particularly those requiring a better understanding of the Internet industry in China.

ShinJoung Yeo is Assistant Professor of Media Studies at Queens College, City University of New York. Her research focuses on the political economy of communication and information centered around labor, policy, and geopolitics. She has published several works including "Tech Companies and Public Health Care in the Ruins of COVID," "Access Now, but for Whom and at What Cost?," "Artists in Tech Cities," "Science and Engineering in Digital Capitalism," and "From Paper Mill to Google Data Center."

Global Media Giants

Series editors: Benjamin J. Birkinbine, Rodrigo Gomez, and Janet Wasko

Since the second half of the 20th century, the significance of media corporate power has been increasing in different and complex ways around the world; the power of these companies in political, symbolic, and economic terms has been a global issue and concern. In the 21st century, understanding media corporations is essential to understanding the political, economic, and socio-cultural dimensions of our contemporary societies.

The **Global Media Giants** series continues the work that began in the series editors' book *Global Media Giants*, providing detailed examinations of the largest and most powerful media corporations in the world.

Vivendi
A Key Player in Global Entertainment and Media
Philippe Bouquillion

Alibaba
Infrastructuring Global China
Hong Shen

Bertelsmann
A Transnational Media Service Giant
Mandy Tröger and Jörg Becker

Baidu
Geopolitical Dynamics of the Internet in China
ShinJoung Yeo

For more information about this series, please visit: https://www.routledge.com/Global-Media-Giants/book-series/GMG

Baidu

Geopolitical Dynamics of the Internet in China

ShinJoung Yeo

Routledge
Taylor & Francis Group
NEW YORK AND LONDON

First published 2023
by Routledge
605 Third Avenue, New York, NY 10158

and by Routledge
4 Park Square, Milton Park, Abingdon, Oxon, OX14 4RN

Routledge is an imprint of the Taylor & Francis Group, an informa business

ISBN: 978-1-032-03564-2 (hbk)
ISBN: 978-1-032-03954-1 (pbk)
ISBN: 978-1-003-18989-3 (ebk)

DOI: 10.4324/9781003189893

Typeset in Times New Roman
by codeMantra

For James

Contents

Figures

Acknowledgments

There is no academic endeavor without collective effort. I'm extremely grateful for Tang Min and Hong Shen who kindly read the full manuscript and offered me insightful feedback. I deeply respect their critical scholarship in the field and am fortunate to have them as friends and colleagues. I'm especially indebted to Tang Min whose generosity, feedback, and questions greatly improved this project. Thanks to Dan Schiller who sent me numerous articles and encouraged me to think about needed scholarship in the midst of today's ongoing crisis. I much appreciate the unbilled lunch sessions with Richard Maxwell discussing research and dealing with my stress and anxiety. Thanks to series editors Benjamin J. Birkinbine, Rodrigo Gomez, and Janet Wasko as well as editorial assistant Emma Sheriff who all kindly understood and supported this work through my family crises. Last but not least, this work wouldn't have gotten finished without James Jacobs who anchors me when I'm adrift and consistently edits my articles and prepositions. There are no words in English to describe in English my gratitude to him (은인 is close).

Introduction

In December, 2020, during the final weeks of the Trump administration, the US considered adding the Chinese search giant Baidu along with Alibaba and Tencent – three of the largest Internet companies in China – to the US's entity list. The entity list functions as an international trade blacklist. It requires a government license for any US company to buy parts and components from foreign companies on the entity list. However, this move was aborted at the last minute. The *Financial Times* reported that the US Treasury Department blocked the Defense and State Departments' attempt because putting the three largest Chinese Internet companies on a blacklist would seriously impact major US investors.[1] According to a 2022 report from the US-China Economic and Security Review Commission, there were 261 Chinese companies listed on US stock exchanges with a total market capitalization of $1.3 trillion.[2] This incident attested to the discordance among different US government agencies on policy toward China; but more importantly, it showed the entanglement of Chinese and US political economies in which the Internet sector is at the nexus. Baidu, Alibaba and Tencent (BAT) are China-based multinational tech companies; however, their impact on the political economy is no longer limited to China; rather it affects a broader global market, and in particular, the US economy.

The purpose of this book is to examine Baidu, China's search giant, to illuminate the political economy of the Chinese Internet sector and its dynamic relationship with global capitalism. This book shows that the case of Baidu – which is often referred to as "Chinese Google" in the West – challenges the analytical framework of the battle between authoritarian China versus democratic US. It demonstrates that the Chinese political economy of the Internet, which is intricately interconnected to the global economy, is restructuring what has long been the US-led global capitalism.

DOI: 10.4324/9781003189893-1

US tech giant Google, the gateway to the Internet, dominates the world. But in China, the Chinese-based search company Baidu controls over 80% of the domestic Chinese search market.[3] China is one of only a few exceptions to Google's global dominance – along with South Korea and Russia – where a local search engine has succeeded in outpacing Google for market dominance. In particular, China – the world's second largest economy and largest Internet market – shows the geopolitical struggle over the global Internet industry, and the contention and collaboration among multinational firms and states to control the most dynamic capitalist economic sector – the Internet.

Baidu is one of the earliest Chinese Internet companies. The company emerged in the early 2000s at a moment when China was in the midst of reforming and converting its economy from a centralized socialist economy to a more market-based economy and was seeking to attract transnational capital in order to build its domestic information and communication technology (ICT) sector as one of its strategic growth industries.[4] From its inception, Baidu was deeply infused with transnational- and particularly US capital; thus, the case of Baidu demonstrates that the growth of the Chinese Internet sector has been deeply hardwired within US-led transnationalized capitalism. This book focuses on the political economy of Baidu as representative of the Chinese Internet sector and delineates a glimpse of the history of coupling between the US and China in which ICTs have been at the core, and the dynamics of China's changing domestic Internet political economy which is being reshaped by contemporary geopolitics and is reshaping the global capitalist system.

To situate Baidu within a broader political economic context, historian Ellen Wood's conceptualization of the current age of capitalism is instructive. Wood writes that today's capitalism is a system in which the economies of capitalist nation states are interconnected and integrated within a global economic system even though the degree of integration varies by nation state.[5] However, the global capitalist system doesn't have one global nation state that administers the system; rather it is a hierarchical and complex system of multiple states. For decades, the US has governed the global capitalist system as a superpower. Meanwhile, each state within the system has had to interact with the US while also having to respond to its own domestic pressures, its own capitalist logics and its own needs, all the while also having to exist within conditions for a global capitalist system.[6] China's reassertion and its ascendence as a political and economic power player has challenged the US-led unipolar global capitalist economic order and prompted US unease over China and its inter-state rivalry. As David Harvey writes, in today's capitalism, competition takes place not only between capitalist firms but also between states that drive technical innovations for capital accumulation.[7] This is the context of the current battle over tech supremacy between the US and China within a global capitalist system. Thus, before discussing the theoretical framework of the political economy of the Internet in China on which this book will be anchored, I will start by providing the geopolitical context within which Baidu's business and the competition between geopolitical rivals China and the US needs to be situated.

Geopolitical Struggle

The Trump administration's hawkish approach toward China in which the US raised tariffs and other trade barriers was seen as a new turning point in the relationship between the two countries dating back to President Richard Nixon's historical travel to Beijing – "the week that changed the world"[8] – in 1972. However, the US has long been trying to realign geopolitics to curtail China's growing economic power. In 2012, the Obama administration's "pivot to Asia" led by then-Secretary of State Hillary Clinton signaled to the world that the US would rebalance regional power in order to prevent China's global political economic influence in the region.[9] Obama's regional strategy was to further engage with the Asian Pacific nations where the increasing power of China could drive away US influence. In particular, China's ascendance in ICT sectoral power in and around the Internet – the backbone of global economic and military power today – spurred US anxiety over its global hegemonic position.

After the Trump administration sharply raised tensions with China, Joe Biden's election anticipated a radical shift from its predecessor; however, the Biden administration's policy toward China has so far adhered to the precedence set by the previous Obama and Trump administrations. Under Biden's mantra "America is back," the US is reshuffling its foreign alliances to rein in China within US-led global capitalist structures. To pursue this goal, the Biden administration shored up its transatlantic tech alliance with the European Union, pushing for joint technical standards and working together in the key technology areas of 5G mobile networks, artificial intelligence (AI), and data flows.[10] The US also forged a new Indo-Pacific AUKUS trilateral security alliance between the US, Great Britain, and Australia to assist Australia in deploying nuclear-powered submarines in the Pacific to counter China – and in the process inadvertently causing a strained relationship with long-time ally France when Australia voided its agreement to buy 12 French diesel-powered submarines and caused France to temporarily recall its ambassadors to the US and Australia.[11] In early 2022, the US and Japan deepened their military ties by signing a new five-year agreement on military-related R&D.

Domestically, in early 2021, the National Security Commission on Artificial Intelligence (NSCAI), led by former Google Chairman Eric Schmidt, released a 700-page report on the impact of AI on defense and national security and warned of vulnerabilities of US AI technology – which has growing impact across major tech sectors including advanced microchip technology – and recommended that the US Congress defend AI against China, tighten up "choke points," and work with allies.[12] President Biden also signed executive order 14017, *America's Supply Chains*, to review a range of supply chain issues, stating "The United States needs resilient, diverse, and secure supply chains to ensure our economic prosperity and national security."[13] Biden's order aimed to tighten control on the digital technology supply chain including chips, batteries, and rare earth and other critical minerals. Moreover, in 2022 the Administration passed the $280 billion dollar bipartisan CHIPS and Science Act[14] – to counter China's growing tech power by subsidizing more than $52 billion in domestic semiconductor production, a major battle ground for tech supremacy between the US and China.[15] The law prohibits subsidized companies from expanding production in China as it is intended to build manufacturing facilities in the US.

As historian Vijay Prashad pointed out, the Trump and Biden administrations have basically followed the precedence set by the Obama administration's "pivot to Asia" policy as the US has been struggling to compete against China's rapid scientific and technological advancements.[16] The US administrations have shared a common goal of attempting to prevent China from undercutting US hegemony in the Asia Pacific region.[17] Noam Chomsky states that US policy toward China is motivated by the perspective that China is a threat to the US led global rules.[18]

Meanwhile, facing increasing hostility and pressure from the US and its allies and with no signs of abating tensions under the Biden administration, the Chinese Communist Party (CCP) is speeding up its new economic development path, focusing on the expansion of the domestic consumption market and the development of core indigenous technological innovations in an attempt to reduce China's reliance on foreign technologies in critical areas, and the reorientation of its economic base away from low-end labor-intensive industries. However, even before the current trade dispute with the US arose, the CCP had already recognized the vulnerability of China's factory-based and highly export-dependent economy.

After the 2008 global financial crisis crashed the US consumer market and collapsed foreign demand, China revived both its domestic economy and the global capitalist economy by injecting $586 billion in infrastructure investment. Equivalent to 13.3% of China's 2008 GDP, this was the largest stimulus in the world.[19] China was the first country to recover; however, the Great Recession also exposed the limitation of China's export-led growth and highlighted the need to move up the global value chains. Despite China's remarkable economic growth in a short period of time, China still relies on foreign suppliers for critical component technologies such as semiconductors – with only 16% produced in China and only half of those manufactured by Chinese companies.[20]

To alleviate its exposure, the CCP has been promoting a new development model under the premise of its "Innovation-Driven Development Strategy (IDDS)" and is moving into capital intensive areas within its high tech sectors.[21] IDDS was introduced in the 13th Five-Year Plan (FYP) (2015–2020) which laid out the strategic emerging industries as new engines of economic growth – including Internet of Things (IoT), Artificial Intelligence (AI), cloud computing, big data, astronautics, biomedicine, robotics, electric vehicles (EVs), autonomous vehicles (AVs), and smart manufacturing – as core technologies to be supported by the state.[22] To implement IDDS, the CCP introduced a series of tech-centered industrial policies – "Made in China 2025" (2015), followed by the "New Generation Artificial Intelligence Development Plan" in 2017 and "Internet Plus" in 2019 – to promulgate next-generation technologies and restructure China's entire industrial base. After the announcement of the 13th FYP, China's R&D expenditure doubled.[23] In 2018, China spent $468 billion, behind only the US and its $582 billion invested in R&D.[24]

The themes of the 13th FYP continued; but with the intensification of the trade dispute with the US, IDDS was accelerated and became the main road map for China's 14th FYP for 2021–2025. However, unlike earlier plans, the 14th FYP has not specificized the China's GDP growth target, stressing instead "high-quality," "people-centered" development and domestic consumption yet promoting to deepen reforms and open up to foreign capital and foreign investment.[25] Echoing the 14th FYP, President Xi cast the slogan of "common prosperity" at the 10th meeting of the Central Committee for Financial and Economic Affairs in 2021 and called to "regulate excessively high incomes and encourage high-income groups and enterprises to return more to society."[26] The CCP's 14th FYP agenda signaled a response not only to the new geopolitical environment but also to changing domestic political economic conditions.

China enjoyed double-digit economic growth for decades, but its economic growth has been declining, with a growth rate of 7.85% in 2012, and in 2018 it even dropped below 7%.[27] In 2020, with the global economy shrinking due to the pandemic, China's GDP grew only 2.2%, its lowest in more than four decades.[28] Furthermore, China has become the second largest economy behind the US and remarkedly lifted 800 million of its people from poverty; however, the wealth gap between rich and poor and urban and rural is still striking. China's top 1% earners hold more wealth than the bottom 50%,[29] and the income gap between rural and urban areas has widened by 57%.[30] There are still 600 million workers who are earning $154 or less a month[31] while the number of Chinese billionaires outpaced the US in 2020.[32] The Chinese party-state has to address this for its legitimacy and the 14th FYP seems to underscore this political economic condition as it has embarked on China's new paradigm-shifting stage of development – "people-centered" and "high-quality" development.

Under the umbrella of "Dual Circulation" strategy, the 14th FYP prioritizes innovation and network technologies as a driving force to expand China's domestic markets (domestic circulation) while pursuing supply side structural reforms to secure critical supply chains and upgrading industrial sectors (external circulation).[33] To pursue this development goal, the Chinese party state is backing digital initiatives including public investment of $1.4 trillion over six years for digital infrastructure in order to absorb next-generation technologies such as 5G, AI, IoT applications, blockchain, big data, and cloud computing and applying them to traditional manufacturing sectors.[34]

This is a shift from the past decades of Chinese industrial policy that supported consumer-facing Internet technologies like social media, e-commerce, online food delivery, etc. The People's

Republic of China (PRC)'s new economic development phase targets capital-intensive industrial applications of the industrial Internet to transform its industrial sectors.[35] To accelerate its implementation, Beijing is drawing in and stimulating private companies like Baidu, Tencent, Alibaba, and others which already have capital, industrial-sized R&D capacity, advanced technologies, talent, and large-scale network infrastructures.

With this as backdrop, the PRC's reassertion into its tech sectors could be seen as threatening private enterprise; the PRC's recent introduction of antitrust and data security regulatory actions against its tech sectors doesn't mean that the CCP is undercutting its private sectors or trying to nationalize and turn them into state-owned companies. However, the new swath of regulatory measures offers several functions for the CCP. Legal scholar Angela Zhang argues that the PRC is nudging the Chinese tech giants to reorient their businesses toward China's industrial sectors rather than consumer-oriented businesses.[36] The jolt has also brought adjustments in the Chinese tech sector which lays ground for new regulatory frameworks to facilitate China's new phase of economic development.[37] President Xi, at an October, 2021 meeting of Communist Party officials, vowed to develop core technologies and network infrastructures that connect all aspects of the economy, promote fair market competition by strengthening regulations to expand China's digital economy, and showed CCP's willingness to address wealth concentration in China.[38] At the same time, President Xi's economic adviser Vice-Premier Liu He affirmed that private firms would need to play a vital role in national development and that the CCP will back its private tech sectors.[39] Liu stated, "there are no changes in the principles and policies for supporting the development of the private economy; they have not changed now and will not change in the future" and assured that the state would create the conditions where private firms and entrepreneurship in the digital economy could flourish.[40]

The PRC emphasizes the role of innovation, regulations, markets, as well as "common prosperity" as parts of its new economic development. This has driven the Chinese tech giants to expand their philanthropic donations, pouring tens of millions into social projects in the areas of education, health, agricultural technology, and poverty alleviation.[41] Whether China is able to prioritize the common good over prosperity for a few or people over markets by utilizing the private sectors remains to be seen; yet, there is evidence that the Chinese state is reforming its existing economic industrial base to gain a better position for itself within the global capitalist system. This is the political economic context in which the search giant Baidu operates today.

Political Economy of the Chinese Internet

There are a number of critical scholars who have foregrounded the study of the political economy of the Internet in China and delineated the role of ICTs in China's restructuring political economy and reintegration into the global capitalist economy. Yuezhi Zhao's work is important in opening up the debate around media and communication in China as Zhao has challenged the state-centered and liberal framework, instead underscoring the state's active participation in absorbing foreign capital and collaborating with transnational media and its ability to negotiate specific terms of entry with transnational capital.[42]

Building on Zhao's work, Yu Hong's expansive empirical work contests the binary framework of state vs market.[43] Hong demonstrates how the state is entangled with market forces and is involved at multifaceted levels both domestically and globally in reshaping Chinese ICTs – one of the main driving forces of China's political economy. Over the past three decades, the Chinese state has developed its network economy at the center of the country's restructuring political economy, with ongoing negotiation and increasing interaction with the global capitalist system. Hong shows that, in converging with global capitalism, the state-led digital capitalism is constantly responding to both private and public actors, transnational and national interests and other broader social forces while trying to create space to maneuver its own self-determination.

To understand the relationship between the state and transnational capital in the development of China's domestic Internet sector, Min Tang documents the state's policy processes of implementing carefully crafted multi-tiered regulations throughout different developmental stages.[44] Tang observes that foreign direct investment (FDI) was unevenly distributed as the restrictions of foreign capital were varied by IT industry and the majority of FDI was funneled into the ICT manufacturing sector. In the 1990s, with the lack of domestic capital, Chinese tech start-ups turned to foreign venture capital. Driven by the first dot.com boom, foreign capital invested in Chinese start-ups as China's Internet sector and global financial capital converged. Tang's work on the political economic case study of Tencent reaffirms that from early on, Chinese-based transnational company Tencent absorbed transnational capital which helped it to weave its myriad businesses into the global Internet market.[45] Chinese tech companies have transnationalized by deeply plugging into the global financial network. Tang's more recent extensive work on the history of the coupling between the US and China is vital to understanding the current conflict between China and the US over the global tech sector. Tang delineates the financialization of the Chinese ICT sector with crossover investment which has changed the structure of China's political economy.[46]

Lianrui Jia shows the close relationship between Chinese Internet companies and global financial institutions, exercising structural power over the companies, and defies the perception of the Chinese Internet as an enclosed state-backed "Chinese Internet."[47] As Chinese companies increasingly operate in the global market, the mainstream media portrays China's "rise" or "takeover" as a new threat to the current US-dominated geopolitical order. However, drawing attention to China's "going out" strategies, Hong Shen underlines the tensions, conflicts, and strategic alliances between the Chinese state's territorial logic and China's homegrown Internet capital's imperative to expand into the global market.[48] These works of critical political economy of the Chinese Internet offer important analytical frameworks to understanding the dynamics of the contemporary Chinese Internet industry that is interlinked to global capitalism and the tensions between state policy, and domestic and transnational capital in which Baidu is situated. Building on these scholarly works, this book will examine the political economy of Baidu which illustrates the rise of Baidu and the dynamics of different units of capital and state in shaping the Chinese Internet market.

The book is comprised of four chapters: history, economic profile, political profile, and cultural profile. The first chapter will examine the evolution of Baidu from its origins to its current state as a dominant search company. In particular, this chapter situates Baidu within the political economic conditions in which Baidu has been able to rise to become one of China's major Internet companies. Through the case of Baidu, it shows the role of transnational capital in developing and shaping China's dynamic Internet sector which is deeply coupled into the global capitalist market. The second chapter outlines Baidu's economic profile by looking at its properties, corporate structure, financial profile, and corporate accumulation strategies. In particular, the chapter shows how Baidu has struggled in its core search business, and has had to find new growth markets. This chapter shows that within the highly competitive domestic Internet as well as international markets, Baidu has aggressively cultivated its AI business and has wholeheartedly joined the global AI race. Chapter three is centered on political aspects surrounding Baidu, examining Baidu's corporate ownership and illustrating the transnational nature of the company and Baidu's relationship to the PRC which is implementing the restructuring of its economic base and upgrading its industrial sectors by deploying massive next-generation technologies like AI. The final chapter looks at Baidu's expansion into cultural domains as China has turned culture into an industry. It will explicate how Baidu is deploying the "sharing" culture as a business model, navigating and shaping China's copyright regime, and moving into the cultural sector from books to museums to streaming video services.

The emergence of China's Internet giant Baidu was not a one-off, serendipitous event. Rather, over the past four decades, the Chinese government has transformed the Internet into a pillar industry which is tightly woven into the global financial sector and the US-led capitalist economy. By locating Baidu within this broader global political economic development and geopolitics, this book will delineate how Baidu is operating within the dynamics of the transnationalized Chinese Internet and domestic political economy and the current context of today's "decoupling" and geopolitical tensions.

Notes

1 Demetri Sevastopulo, James Fontanella-Khan and Eric Platt, "Alibaba, Tencent and Baidu spared from US investor blacklist," *Financial Times*, January 31, 2021, https://www.ft.com/content/46505ee0-fb3d-4cf0-a3df-64e9661e839f.

2 U.S-China Economic and Security Review Commission, "Chinese-Companies Listed on Major U.S. Stock Exchanges." March 31, 2022, https://www.uscc.gov/research/chinese-companies-listed-major-us-stock-exchanges.

3 Lai Lin Thomala, "Market share of search engines in China as of December 2021, based on pageview," *Statista*, January 14, 2022, https://www.statista.com/statistics/253340/market-share-of-search-engines-in-china-pageviews/.

4 Min Tang, *Tencent: The Political Economy of China's Surging Internet Giant* (New York: Taylor & Francis, 2019), 9–30.

5 Ellen Meiksins Wood, "Unhappy family," *Monthly Review*, June 1, 1999, https://monthlyreview.org/1999/07/01/unhappy-families/.

6 Ibid.

7 David Harvey, "The coercive laws of competition," Anti-Capitalist Chronicles, November 18, 2021, https://anticapitalistchronicles.libsyn.com/the-coercive-laws-of-competition.

8 Margaret MacMillan, *Nixon and Mao: The Week That Changed the World* (New York: Random House, 2008).

9 Vijay Prashad and Jie Xiong, "Why Xinjiang is central to US cold war on China," *Asia Times*, April 17, 2021, https://asiatimes.com/2021/04/why-xinjiang-is-central-to-us-cold-war-on-china/.

10 Anu Bradford and Raluca Csernatoni, "Toward a strengthened transatlantic technology alliance," Carnegie Endowment for International Peace, January 26, 2021, https://carnegieendowment.org/2021/01/26/toward-strengthened-transatlantic-technology-alliance-pub-83565.

11 Steven Erlanger, "The sharp U.S. Pivot to Asia is throwing Europe off balance," *New York Times*, September 17, 2021, https://www.nytimes.com/2021/09/17/world/europe/biden-china-europe-submarine-deal.html.

12 Final Report National Security Commission on Artificial Intelligence (March 19, 2021), https://www.nscai.gov/wp-content/uploads/2021/03/Full-Report-Digital-1.pdf.

13 Joseph Biden, Executive Order on America's Supply Chains (E.O. 14017), February 24, 2021, https://www.federalregister.gov/documents/2021/03/01/2021-04280/americas-supply-chains.

14 The Act consolidated the House's America COMPETES Act (H.R. 4521) with the Senate's U.S. Innovation and Competition Act (S. 1260) and was combined into H.R. 4346 – Supreme Court Security Funding Act of 2022. See U.S. Congress, House, *Supreme Court Security Funding Act of 2022*, H.R. 4346, 117th Cong., 1st sess. Introduced in House July 1, 2021, https://www.congress.gov/bill/117th-congress/house-bill/4346/text.

15 White House, *FACT SHEET: CHIPS and Science Act Will Lower Costs Create Jobs Strengthen Supply Chains and Counter China*, August 9, 2022, https://www.whitehouse.gov/briefing-room/statements-releases/2022/08/09/fact-sheet-chips-and-science-act-will-lower-costs-create-jobs-strengthen-supply-chains-and-counter-china/.

16 Vijay Prashad and Jie Xiong, "Why Xinjiang is central to US cold war on China," *Asia Times*, April 17, 2021, https://asiatimes.com/2021/04/why-xinjiang-is-central-to-us-cold-war-on-china/.

17 Keikichi Takahashi, "How unique is Trump's China policy?" *The Diplomat*, June 17, 2020, https://thediplomat.com/2020/06/how-unique-is-trumps-china-policy/.

18 Brett Wilkins, "Noam Chomsky warns of 'very dangerous' US antagonism of China," *Canadian Dimension*, December 1, 2021, https://canadiandimension.com/articles/view/noam-chomsky-warns-of-very-dangerous-us-antagonism-of-china.

19 Wayne M. Morrison, "China and the global financial crisis: Implications for the United States," Congressional Research Service, June 3, 2009, https://sgp.fas.org/crs/row/RS22984.pdf.

20 James Andrew Lewis, "China's pursuit of semiconductor independence," Center for Strategic & International Studies, February 27, 2019, https://www.csis.org/analysis/chinas-pursuit-semiconductor-independence.

21 Central Committee of the Communist Party of China, Outline of the National Innovation-Driven Development Strategy, trans. Etcetera Language Group, Inc. (Center for Security and Emerging Technology, 2019), https://cset.georgetown.edu/publication/outline-of-the-national-innovation-driven-development-strategy/.
22 Katherine Koleski, *The 13th Five-Year Plan*, U.S.-China Economic and Security Review Commission, February 14, 2017, https://www.uscc.gov/sites/default/files/Research/The%2013th%20Five-Year%20Plan_Final_2.14.17_Updated%20(002).pdf.
23 Dennis Normile, "China again boosts R&D spending by more than 10%," *Science*, August 28, 2020, https://www.science.org/content/article/china-again-boosts-rd-spending-more-10.
24 Ibid.
25 Outline of the People's Republic of China 14th Five-Year Plan for National Economic and Social Development and Long-Range Objectives for 2035, trans, *Xinhua News Agency*, March 12, 2021, https://cset.georgetown.edu/wp-content/uploads/t0284_14th_Five_Year_Plan_EN.pdf.
26 Phillip Inman, "Chinese president vows to 'adjust excessive incomes' of super rich," *Guardian,* August 18, 2021, https://www.theguardian.com/world/2021/aug/18/chinese-president-xi-jinping-vows-to-adjust-excessive-incomes-of-super-rich.
27 C. Textor, "Growth rate of real gross domestic product (GDP) in China from 2011 to 2021 with forecasts until 2026," *Statista*, February 16, 2022, https://www.statista.com/statistics/263616/gross-domestic-product-gdp-growth-rate-in-china/.
28 Stella Qiu and Kevin Yao, "China sets 'low bar' for GDP growth, pledges more jobs," *Reuters*, March 4, 2021, https://www.reuters.com/article/us-china-parliament-gdp/china-sets-low-bar-for-gdp-growth-pledges-more-jobs-idUSKBN2AX03L.
29 Sharon Chen, "China has a huge wealth-gap problem – and it's getting worse," *Bloomberg*, December 24, 2020, https://www.bloomberg.com/news/storythreads/2020-12-24/china-has-a-huge-wealth-gap-problem-and-it-s-getting-worse.
30 Shin Watanabe, "China's income inequality grows despite village modernization," *Nikkei Asia*, June 13, 2021, https://asia.nikkei.com/Economy/China-s-income-inequality-grows-despite-village-modernization.
31 Ryan Hass, "Assessing China's 'common prosperity' campaign," *Brookings*, September 9, 2021, https://www.brookings.edu/blog/order-from-chaos/2021/09/09/assessing-chinas-common-prosperity-campaign/.
32 James Kynge "Xi Jinping takes aim at the gross inequalities of China's 'gilded age'" *Financial Times* August 20, 2021, https://www.ft.com/content/8761f611-5619-4c2d-8627-577ba9359cd4.
33 Ibid.
34 U.S. Library of Congress, Congressional Research Service, *China's 14th Five-Year Plan: A First Look*, by Karen M. Sutter, Specialist and Michael D. Sutherlan, IF11684 (2021), https://crsreports.congress.gov/product/pdf/IF/IF11684.

35 Matt Sheehan, "China Technology 2025: Fragile Tech Superpower," *Marco Polo*, October 26, 2020, https://macropolo.org/analysis/china-technology-forecast-2025-fragile-tech-superpower/.
36 Angela Huyue Zhang, *Chinese Antitrust Exceptionalism* (Oxford: Oxford University Press, 2021).
37 Kai von Carnap and Valarie Tan, "Tech regulation in China brings in sweeping changes," *Merics*, November 3, 2021, https://merics.org/en/short-analysis/tech-regulation-china-brings-sweeping-changes.
38 "Xi Eyes Innovation, Oversight to Grow China's Digital Economy," *Bloomberg News*, October 19, 2021, https://www.bloomberg.com/news/articles/2021-10-19/china-s-xi-vows-tighter-oversight-of-tech-firms-digital-economy.
39 Orange Wang, "China's Xi Jinping, Liu He move to reassure private sector as Beijing's Big Tech crackdown rattles entrepreneurs," *South Morning China*, September 6, 2021, https://www.scmp.com/economy/china-economy/article/3147764/chinas-xi-jinping-liu-he-move-reassure-private-sector.
40 "China's Liu He assures business of support, amid regulatory crackdown," *Reuters*, September 6, 2021, https://www.reuters.com/world/china/chinas-liu-he-says-support-private-business-has-not-changed-2021-09-06/.
41 Daniel Slotta, "Announced donations to combat coronavirus from tech giants in China 2020," *Statista*, February 21, 2022, https://www.statista.com/statistics/1106335/china-covid-19-tech-companies/; Daniel Tam-Claiborne, "Chinese tech philanthropy in the age of 'common prosperity'," SupChina, November 23, 2021, https://supchina.com/2021/11/23/chinese-tech-philanthropy-in-the-age-of-common-prosperity/.
42 Yuezhi Zhao, *Communication in China: Political Economy, Power, and Conflict* (Lanham, MD: Rowman & Littlefield, 2008), 138–148.
43 Yu Hong, *Networking China: The Digital Transformation of the Chinese Economy* (Champaign: University of Illinois Press, 2017).
44 Min Tang, "From 'bring-in' to 'going out': Transnationalizing China's Internet Capital' through State Policies," *Chinese Journal of Communication*, 13, no. 1 (2019): 27–47.
45 Min Tang, *Tencent: The Political Economy of China's Surging Internet Giant* (Taylor & Francis, 2019).
46 Min Tang, "Not Yet the End of Transnational Digital Capitalism: A Communication Perspective of the U.S.–China Decoupling Rhetoric," *International Journal of Communication*, 16 (2021): 1506–1531.
47 Lianrui Jia, "Going Public and Going Global: Chinese Internet Companies and Global Finance Networks," *Westminster Paper in Communication and Culture*, 13, no. 1 (2018): 17–36.
48 Shen Hong, *Across the Great (Fire) Wall: China and the Global Internet* (PhD. Diss., University of Illinois Urbana Champaign, 2017).

1 History

This chapter examines the rise and development of Baidu within the political economic context in which the Chinese domestic Internet industry was established. It demonstrates that the major Internet companies in China have grown by integrating themselves within the global capitalist system as the People's Republic of China (PRC) created conditions to attract and control foreign capital on the one hand and established China's dynamic domestic Internet industry on the other. The chapter shows that the growth of Baidu as a dominant search engine in China took place within the process of increasing interdependence of the political economy between the US and China, particularly centered around the most dynamic sector of the Internet, and China's reintegration into the global capitalist economy.

To understand the emergence of Baidu as a dominant search engine, Min Tang's three phrases of integration between the US and China through the ICT sector are instructive to situate Baidu within the broader scope of China's development of its Internet industry.[1] The first stage was China's opening up in the 1970s and 1980s when China and the US signed a bilateral trade agreement reopening diplomatic relations after 29 years; the second stage in the 1990s and early 2000s accelerated the integration of the two countries' economies through goods, financial capital and labor; the third stage is the era of the post-2008 economic crisis when the role of China's global economy was elevated and the economically-entangled relationship between China and the US was illuminated. The first stage provided the foreground for relinking between China and the US through China's ICTs sectors. Baidu was established and grew in the second stage when China's Internet start-ups began to pop up, drew in foreign and in particular US venture capital, and increasingly became integrated into global financial markets. I call the second stage of the relationship between China and the US as "the age of accelerated coupling."

DOI: 10.4324/9781003189893-2

The Age of Accelerated Coupling

With the Trump administration's deepening tensions between China and the US – which have largely been maintained if not exacerbated by the Biden administration – there has been talk of "decoupling" or the disintegration of the US economy from China among policy-makers, business people, and scholars.[2] In 2021, the US Chamber of Commerce released a 92-page document on the issues surrounding any proposed US–China decoupling, illustrating how the US and Chinese economies have been deeply integrated and the fault lines that would be created with any possible separation.[3] The main focus of the document is about the Internet and the new generation of technologies which have been interwoven into the global supply chains and their implications on the disentanglement of the two economies.[4] As Tang documented, the decades of integration between the US and China has resulted in the deep interdependence from hardware to software to capital investment.[5] The Chinese Internet sector grew out of this so-called "coupling" between the US and China.

In 1978, at the third Plenary Session of the 11th Central Committee of the Chinese Communist Party (CCP), the PRC officially announced its commitment to Deng Xiaoping's "Open Door" policy. The Mao era had centralized economic policy focusing on social development which was followed by Deng's "openness" and market-oriented economic reforms.[6] In the early reform era, the CCP prioritized its information and communication sectors (ICTs) as a new driving force of economic growth. In the 1980s, China rapidly expanded its telecommunication network infrastructure, and subsequently, adopted IT in general as part of its national economic development. China's strategy to boost its IT sectors has intertwined with China's reintegration into US-led digital capitalism and has selectively targeted transnational capital to fund this strategy.[7]

The CCP attracted substantial foreign direct investment (FDI) as it shifted its economy toward market-oriented and information-driven development. China's accession into the World Trade Organization (WTO) in 2001 was seen as an official juncture of China's opening up to foreign capital; however, long before that, the Chinese government facilitated various forms of foreign investment – joint ventures, contractual arrangements, equity investments, and foreign R&D investments – in the development of its ICT sectors.[8] Dan Schiller and Yuezhi Zhao described this as a new phase of expansion of market logics and transnationalized capitalist development.[9]

To draw in and accommodate foreign capital, the PRC actively created the legal conditions for its burgeoning foreign investment environment and implemented a series of regulations – including the Joint Venture Enterprise Law of 1979, the Foreign Capital Enterprise Law of 1986, and the Chinese-Foreign Cooperative Enterprise Law of 1988 – to attract foreign capital as well as to give Chinese companies an avenue to access advanced technologies.[10] This was followed by the formation of foreign Special Economic Zones (SEZ) which were not only export zones but also used as hubs to draw in foreign capital and technical inflow into China. By the end of 1990, the total number of agreements with foreign investors within the designated SEZs had grown from 949 in 1982 to 29,693, growing from $6.01 billion to $68.1 billion in FDI.[11]

Along with a favorable legal environment for foreign capital, China launched a series of national science and technology initiatives – among them the National High-tech R&D "863 Program" and the Ministry of Science and Technology's (MOST) Torch Program – which facilitated the growth of domestic high-tech start-ups in the 1980s with funding and innovation clusters to develop indigenous technologies.[12] Concomitantly, the central government began to develop venture capital by leveraging R&D institutions and universities, with the Torch program and banks financing spin-off projects. However, these programs had limitations and weren't able to scale up to finance new tech ventures to achieve broader long-term national economic development goals.[13] By the 1990s, the PRC had shifted its venture capital system from government-led to commercial activities establishing domestic venture firms to speed up commercialization of technologies. Local governments funded the establishment of domestic Government Venture Capital Firms (GVCFs) and university-backed VC firms in major provinces and cities like Quandong and Shanghai.[14]

Despite the central government's efforts, when Chinese Internet start-ups began to emerge in the late 1990s, there still wasn't sufficient domestic capital to fund China's burgeoning Internet start-ups. Moreover, as Min Tang pointed out, FDI initially preferred to invest in the manufacturing sector where return on investment was more guaranteed while the Internet service sectors were still under the radar.[15] Thus, Chinese Internet tech start-ups had few options, and they turned to foreign and US venture capital which had been searching for new sites of investment after the dot-com crash.

By 2001, 8 of the top 10 venture capital firms and 14 of the top 20 in China were foreign venture firms.[16]

Venture capital and joint ventures were the common financing model for Chinese tech start-ups. However, since the early 2000s, Chinese start-ups also exploited the so-called "variable interest entity" (VIE) to tap into global capital and bypass the Chinese law that limited foreign investment in value-added Chinese Internet services and telecommunication. It was illegal for Chinese Internet companies to have any non-Chinese shareholders, but the VIE structure had created a loophole that enabled Chinese companies to establish offshore entities for overseas stock market listings and had drawn in foreign investors by allowing them to buy stock in Chinese tech companies. VIEs also provided global capital with access to the bourgeoning Chinese Internet market through inter-capital collaboration. Chinese and foreign investors long understood that the VIE structure sat in a legally gray area; however, they were willing to take the risk in order to gain access to the massive and fast-growing market.[17] Chinese tech companies' use of VIE wasn't a secret; however, the PRC maintained its ambiguous policy stance and never declared VIEs to be illegal nor attempted to clamp down on the system and practice. Looked at from the Western perspective, why then did US investors continue to invest in Chinese Internet firms in this manner? There was a mutual understanding among the transnational capitalist class that the Chinese state would be unlikely to take any measures that would negatively affect China's major Internet firms.[18]

The Birth of Baidu

With this context as backdrop, Baidu was founded by Eric Xu and Robin Li in the Zhongguancun, Beijing tech hub in January 2000. Li and Xu are Chinese nationals and both were educated in the US. Current CEO Li studied computer science at the State University of New York (SUNY) at Buffalo and worked at Dow Jones and as a search engine engineer at Infoseek in Silicon Valley, an early search engine firm partly owned by Disney at that time. Li developed the RankDex, a site ranking algorithm which later was awarded a US patent.[19] Eric Xu received his PhD in biology from Texas A&M University and had personal contacts with Yahoo!'s John Wu among other prominent Chinese nationals in Silicon Valley.[20] Li and Xu took their idea to the Valley, quickly raised $1.2 million from Peninsula Capital and Integrity Partner and returned to China.[21]

Like many early Chinese Internet start-ups, Baidu received seed money from Silicon Valley venture capital firms.[22] Baidu had its Initial Public Offering (IPO) in 2005. It was considered the biggest opening on NASDAQ since the dot.com peak of 2000, soon securing capital from two other major US venture capital firms, Draper Fisher Jurvetson (DFJ) and IDG Technology Venture.[23] The US–China Economic and Security Review Commission's 2010 Annual Report to Congress revealed that Baidu's majority investors were Americans and American firms – including Google! – as US investors were eyeing the quickly growing Chinese Internet market.[24] Google bought 749,625 Baidu shares for $5 million and later expressed an interest in acquiring Baidu.[25] Baidu welcomed Google's investment. Li stated, "Google is a leader in the global Internet industry and its investment will help investors appreciate the value of a search engine provider like Baidu."[26]

At the time Baidu was filing its IPO, more than 45% of the company was owned by foreign institutional investors.[27] In fact, Google tried to acquire Baidu, offering $1.6 billion to gain control over the Chinese search market, but ultimately Baidu rejected Google's takeover attempt.[28] Rebuffed by Baidu, Google instead decided to launch Google China to try and seize the largest Internet market in the world. By the time Baidu began its operations in 2001, other commercial portals like NetEase.com, Sina.com, and Sohu.com were already established in China and attracting significant web traffic. Besides domestic Internet companies, Yahoo! and Google were also providing several services and trying to carve out their market share. Thus, there was no guarantee that Baidu would succeed. How then was Baidu able to gain web traffic and win over users from local web portals as well as global brands Yahoo! and Google?

The common explanation in the Western media was that the success of Baidu and other Chinese Internet giants was due to their compliance with the PRC's censorship rules along with direct protection from the Chinese state. There is no question that the CCP created favorable conditions for its domestic companies; however, the growth of Baidu also needs to be explained within the dynamics of inter-capitalist competition that manifested in China's evolving IP regimes, and technical and local market conditions.

At first, Baidu provided search service for other companies. But in 2001, Baidu decided to pursue being an independent search engine and offered bidding to advertisers for space on its site. To kick off its search business, Baidu offered an MP3 music search service aimed at younger users as a strategy to attract new users because a general search service alone wasn't sufficient to compete against other existing Internet sites. This was a risky move for Baidu because of the high likelihood that the music industry would go after Baidu for IP infringement.[29] To dodge legal issues, Baidu didn't upload MP3 files to its own servers but only provided links to MP3 files on other sites. Competing against Baidu, Yahoo! China also provided MP3 music services. According to its 2005 annual report, 16% of Baidu's traffic was coming from its MP3 search service.[30]

The legally fluid area of copyright in China at that time initially provided Baidu and Yahoo! time to increase their user base over the first few years of their operations. However, Baidu was soon entangled in numerous copyright lawsuits. In 2005, Baidu was sued for copyright infringement by the International Federation of the Phonographic Industry (IFPI) on behalf of seven major music labels including Universal, EMI, Warner, Sony BMG, and their local subsidiaries Gold Label (EMI), Cinepoly, and Go East.[31] In response, Baidu argued that the search engine was a platform treating music files like any other information on the Internet. Initially, the Beijing First Intermediate Court found that since Baidu was not hosting files, the company was not liable for copyright infringement. In 2006, the IFPI also went after Yahoo! China for linking to music files. The Beijing court reversed its decision from the Baidu case and found Yahoo! China guilty of copyright infringement.[32] In 2008, Baidu along with Sohu was again sued by Sony BMG Music Entertainment (Hong Kong) Ltd., Universal Music Ltd., and Warner Music Hong Kong for copyright infringement which brought it once again before the Beijing First Intermediate People's Court.[33] In 2010, the court once again favored Baidu, arguing that linking to their party content did not constitute copyright infringement. On appeal, three music companies took the case to Beijing Higher People's Court, but they later reached a settlement outside the court.[34]

On the surface, these cases could be seen as a fight between Baidu and the music industry, but this was also part of a larger digital trade dispute between the US and China. The office of the US Trade Representative had listed Baidu under "notorious markets" for several years for facilitating piracy and counterfeiting.[35] Interestingly, despite the Beijing court siding with Baidu, the company decided to settle with the music companies. US pressure might have been one of the factors in Baidu's decision to settle, but as Dong Han astutely points out, the CCP, which began to promote the growth of its cultural industry, was already shifting toward strengthening its copyright regime as part of its market-oriented reforms and allying with the US IP regime.[36] In 2011, Baidu finally ended years of legal squabbles and signed a joint venture agreement between Universal Music Group, Warner Music Group, and Sony BMG to license over 500,000 songs in their catalogs.[37]

In addition to Baidu's maneuvering around early copyright laws, the company was also well versed in local conditions. According to Kai-Fu Lee, the former president of Google China, Baidu was able to win over users by localizing its services – Google was unable to maneuver between local differences and adjust to technical changes. Lee argued that Americans used search engines like the Yellow Pages, but Chinese users treated search engines more like online shopping sites where users look at different things and pick one.[38] In fact, Google built its search platform to draw as many users as it could and quickly push them away from the site. However, like a portal site, Baidu opened its search results in a new browser, so that when users clicked on a link, they were encouraged to stick around the search site. Lee lamented that Google China was reluctant to modify its code in response to Chinese user behavior because it was a challenge to technically maintain at that time and Google's superior algorithm was considered sufficient to win over Chinese users.[39]

However, drawing in users was not sufficient for a search engine to increase its advertising revenue. Baidu needed to find clients to sell its keywords. Google designed an automated ads selling process and offered its self-service ads platform payable with credit cards. In the US, this allowed Google to reduce labor costs and quickly scale up its ads selling. However, the environment in the China of 2001 was very different. Most advertisers were small or medium-sized enterprises who weren't Internet users and had no credit cards for online payments. Thus, Baidu had to build a large-sized sales force going door to door, making cold calls, and teaching potential clients how to use their system. Because of this reality, the company was able through massive effort to gain market share gradually over time. Baidu cultivated its initial ads market by deploying labor-intensive sales pitches, while Google had only a limited number of sale agents.[40]

As part of its accumulation and competition strategy, Baidu was also aggressively building partnerships with foreign as well as other booming domestic IT companies. For foreign companies, strategic agreements with Baidu were a way to break into the Chinese information market. In 2006, Baidu struck a deal with MTV to provide television and music content to Baidu. The company teamed up with Providence equity partners – one of Hulu's investors – to inject $50 million into the creation of the licensed online video platform iQiyi.com,[41] established a joint venture with Japan-based Rakuten to operate a Business-to-Consumer (B2C) online shopping service in the Chinese market, entered into a cooperative agreement with Nokia, and worked with Intel to develop search services for home PCs, laptops, and mobile phones. Baidu also allied with Dell, Inc. to develop tablet computers and mobile phones to target the Chinese market that was at the time dominated by Apple and Chinese company Lenovo. Soon after Google "withdrew" from China in 2010 amidst a cyberattack on its servers and a dispute over censorship of its search results – Google didn't fully withdraw because the company's ads business still operates in China catering to Chinese companies targeting the international markets[42] – Baidu and Microsoft search engine Bing formed an alliance so that Bing could provide Baidu's English search results on its platform.[43] Bing still operates in China with a little over 4.4% market share and has for the last several years been expanding its cloud business.[44] By partnering with foreign Internet players, Baidu strategically integrated into the global Internet sphere and increasingly raised its domestic market share.

In 2005, Baidu's search engine had captured 52% of the market; Google was second with 33%; Sohu.com had 4.6% of the market; Sina had 4%; and Yahoo! China had a 3.7% share.[45] When Google partially pulled out from mainland China, Baidu's market share jumped to 64% and Google's share declined from 35% previous year to 30%.[46] The Western mainstream media predicted that Baidu would exclusively dominate China's search market with Chinese government policies supporting Chinese-owned companies. Indeed, after Google's partial departure, Baidu seemed to secure its dominant position over the Internet. However, the Chinese search market has proven to be dynamic and fluid, with new contenders drawing in US and other foreign capital. This fluidity has caused Baidu to struggle to compete against its many domestic private and public competitors.

Inter-Capital Rivalries

As search became a lucrative segment of the Chinese Internet market, several new search companies began flocking into the burgeoning market. This was led by Baidu's usual competitors Tencent and Alibaba as well as state-owned media companies which were under much pressure from the CCP to generate profit.

The search market was quickly crowded with new competitors. Qihoo was founded by former Yahoo! China Executive Zhou Hongyi[47] and was initially backed by the venture capital firm Sequoia Capital[48]; Sogou was launched by Sohu, the first Chinese language search engine/portal with seed capital from MIT media lab director Nicholas Negroponte – the One Laptop per Child (OLPC) evangelist – and Edward Roberts of MIT's Sloan School of Management; and Tencent's search engine Soso, which later backed Sogou's IPO and merged with Sogou.[49]

Moreover, in 2017, Tencent introduced its internal app search engine *WeChat Search*. Unlike traditional search, WeChat Search doesn't access the entire web but rather is confined to the content within WeChat's walled garden. Without leaving WeChat, users can search for and access a vast amount of information including weather, stocks, medical consultations, and entertainment. Tencent has blocked Baidu from indexing its WeChat content generated by its 1.2 billion users. Acquiring Sogou would allow Tencent to turn into a full-blown search engine in its own right.

E-commerce giant Alibaba also heavily invested in the search market. In 2005, the company signed an exclusive deal with Yahoo! acquiring Yahoo! China's operations including its search technology. In return, Yahoo! invested $1 billion for a 40% stake in Alibaba. With fresh new capital from Yahoo!, Alibaba was able to compete against Baidu in the search market; the company wouldn't allow Baidu to crawl its e-commerce site, a strategy to avoid Baidu functioning as a middleman between consumers and Alibaba.[50] Alibaba also sought to tackle China's mobile search market, and formed a joint venture called *Shenma* in 2014 with Chinese browser developer UCWeb. Shenma was touted as a "mobile first" search engine.

With the explosion of mobile use in China, Baidu in 2011 launched its own android-based mobile OS Baidu Yi, embedding its own services and teaming up with Dell to build Yi OS-based mobile phones; however, its high-profile mobile venture failed as the Yi-based phones weren't able to compete against Apple and Lenovo. As its competitors encroached on the search domain, Baidu also moved into a range of adjacent Internet markets. Similar to the US market, as Chinese Internet firms diversify their accumulation strategies, they move into each other's territories of search, social media, browsers, mobile phones, music, games, video, and e-commerce, all predicated on continuing commodification and commercialization of the Internet. For both defensive and offensive purposes, Baidu established a range of vertical channels by acquiring 40% of e-book sellers, a travel-booking service (Qunar.com), e-commerce sites (Yougou.com, 360buy.com, tg.com.cn, yaodian100.com), an online community (jingtime.com) and a housing information portal (anjuke.com).[51]

While China's private Internet companies were competing with each other, there are other contenders to Baidu that were barely on the Western media's radar – specifically Chinese party state information service outlets. With the bourgeoning Internet market, state capital was pressured to expand its own operations onto the Internet in an attempt to increase revenues by injecting more private capital into its businesses.[52]

The People's Daily started to build its online operations in 1997 when it launched *People's Daily Online* which was partially owned by state-owned telecommunication companies – China Mobile, China Union, and China Telecom. The newspaper's Internet venture was primarily viewed as the Chinese party state's effort to propagate its party agenda through news media, but it was equally a business as a commercialized press was seen as imperative to coping with the shifting information industry. In 2010, as part of an effort to expand its private capital, *People's Daily* also built its own news search engine called Jike, hoping to tap into the flourishing search engine ads market. Not surprisingly, Jike was not able to make even a small dent against its domestic competitors. It quickly failed, but the state media relaunched a new search engine called ChinaSo in 2014 by merging Jike and Xinhua's search engine Panguso.[53] ChinaSo has also struggled to make headway in the search market.[54]

People's Daily Online, which released its IPO in Shanghai, didn't shy away from its market-oriented business model to compete against private Internet companies. The company described its business as a "market-oriented" commercial news portal which benefited from transnational capital and expressed that "it needs to accelerate its restructuring drive and 'take active measures' to compete with those commercial rivals."[55] As the state is part of the market, Baidu is not only dealing with its commercial Internet rivals but also competing against state-owned entities.

In the US, Google occupies 88% of the search engine market and 95% of all mobile search.[56] However, China's search market has been much more fragmented as new players continue to enter the market and constantly challenge Baidu's search dominance. As of this writing, Baidu's main revenue source of online ads via search has declined 14% since 2016 as the company faces intense competition on multiple fronts.[57] Recently, ByteDance – backed by Kohlberg Kravis Roberts, SoftBank Group, Sequoia Capital, General Atlantic, and Hillhouse Capital Group, the owner of social media app TikTok – launched its search service Toutiao Search, scooping up technical experts from Google, Bing and Baidu.[58] In response, Ping Xiaoli, general manager of Baidu App stated, "We have estimated that there are about two new players emerging in the search engine market each year."[59] Whether Baidu is able to hold on to its position in the search market is an open question.

Conclusion

The development of Baidu demonstrates that the company emerged as a major Internet player during the age in which the ICTs sector was a vehicle driving the economic coupling between the US and China. The development of the Chinese search engine market evolved in the context in which China was expanding its market economy and Baidu and its competitors – Sogou, Qihoo 360, Tencent's Soso, and Alibaba's mobile search Shenma – grew through the absorption of transnational capital with the state also being a critical actor in transnationalizing the Chinese Internet.

The history of Baidu has challenged the common rhetoric that the growth of the Chinese Internet market was cultivated behind the "Great Fire Wall" managed by the Chinese state which dictates and censors search engines. Baidu grew within the political economic context in which the Internet was considered a strategic industry in which the state, along with domestic and transnational capital dialectically interacted in continuing to shape the Internet industry in China – with the significant sector substantially integrated into the US economy and global capitalism.[60] The current debates on "decoupling" need to be understood within the context of China's global reintegration within which the Internet sector has become the nexus. The decades of the intricate integration between the US and China also limits their maneuverability in a time of conflict, rivalry, clashes of interests, and competition.

China's Internet sector is extremely dynamic and competitive, and Baidu continues to wrestle with its old and new search competitors backed by domestic and transnational capital in order to maintain its dominance in the Internet sector. Baidu's search business is still the main source of its revenue. But it faces major political economic issues with the rise of walled garden super apps like WeChat, its exclusive reliance on the domestic Chinese market, and shifting geopolitical landscape. The next chapter will demonstrate how Baidu is trying to survive via an ever-changing business profile and restructuring into the new growth sector of Artificial Intelligence (AI).

Notes

1 Ming Tang, "Not Yet the End of Transnational Digital Capitalism: A Communication Perspective of the U.S.–China Decoupling Rhetoric," *International Journal of Communication*, 16 (2022): 1506–1531.
2 Frank Lavin, "This is what U.S.-China decoupling looks like," *Forbes*, December 8, 2021, https://www.forbes.com/sites/franklavin/2021/12/08/this-is-what-us-china-decoupling-looks-like/?sh=1461e14c3b39.
3 U.S. Chamber of Commerce, "Understanding U.S. -China decoupling: Macro trends and industry," February 17, 2021, https://www.uschamber.com/assets/archived/images/024001_us_china_decoupling_report_fin.pdf.
4 Ibid.
5 Ming Tang, "Not Yet the End of Transnational Digital Capitalism," 1506–1531.
6 Minqi Li, *China and the 21st Century Crisis* (London: Pluto Press, 2016), 79.
7 Yuezhi Zhao, *Communication in China: Political Economy, Power, and Conflict* (Lanham, MD: Rowman & Littlefield, 2008), 195; Min Tang, "From 'bring-in' to 'going out': Transnationalizing China's Internet Capital' through State Policies," *Chinese Journal of Communication*, 13, no. 1 (2019): 27–47.
8 Yu Hong, Labor, Class Formation, and China's Informationized Policy of Economic Development (Lanham, MD: Lexington Books, 2011), 36–37.
9 Yuezhi Zhao and Dan Schiller, "Dances with Wolves? China's Integration into Digital Capitalism," *Info*, 3, no. 2 (2001): 137–151.
10 Victoria Mantzopoulos and Raphael Shen, *Political Economy of China's Systemic Transformation: 1979 to the Present* (New York: Palgrave Macmillan, 2016), 59–60.
11 Ibid., 57–59.
12 Steven White, Jian Gao and Wei Zang, "Financing New Ventures in China: System Antecedents and Institutionalization," *Research Policy*, 34, no. 6 (2005): 849–913.
13 Ibid.
14 Ibid.
15 Tang, "From 'bring-in' to Going Out," 27–47.
16 Steven White, Jian Gao and Wei Zang, "Financing New Ventures in China: System Antecedents and Institutionalization," *Research Policy* 34, no. 6 (2005): 906.

17 Angela Zhang, *Chinese Antitrust Exceptionalism: How the Rise of China Challenges Global Regulation* (Oxford: Oxford University Press, 2021), 84.
18 Richard Pearson, "Looking at Chinese VIE's," *Forbes*, October 18, 2012, http://www.forbes.com/sites/richardpearson/2012/10/18/looking-at-chinese-vies/.
19 Yanhong Li, "Hypertext document retrieval system and method," US Patent 5920859A, issued July 6, 1999, https://patents.google.com/patent/US5920859A/en?oq=US5920859A.
20 David Barboza, "Web prodigy's secret: He kept on searching – Technology – International Herald Tribune," N*ew York Times*, September 17, 2006, https://www.nytimes.com/2006/09/17/technology/17iht-baidu.2836319.html.
21 Wenxian Zhang, Huiyao Wang, and Ilan Alon, *Entrepreneurial and Business Elites of China: The Chinese Returnees Who Have Shaped Modern China* (Bingley: Emerald, 2011), 86.
22 David Barboza, "The Rise of Baidu," *New York Times*, September 17, 2006, http://www.nytimes.com/2006/09/17/business/yourmoney/17baidu.html?pagewanted=all.
23 Ibid.
24 Report to Congress of the US China Economic and Security Review Commission, 100th Cong., 2nd sess (Washington, DC: US Government Printing Office, 2010), 231, http://origin.www.uscc.gov/sites/default/files/annual_reports/2010-Report-to-Congress.pdf.
25 "Baidu.com Shares Soar in U.S. Debut," *Associated Press*, August 5, 2005, https://www.nbcnews.com/id/wbna8840916.
26 "Google Acquires Sizeable Stake in Baidu," *China Daily*, June 16, 2004, http://www.china.org.cn/english/BAT/98325.htm.
27 Max Parasol, *AI Development and the 'Fuzzy Logic' of Chinese Cyber Security and Data Laws* (Cambridge: Cambridge University Press, 2021), 44.
28 Jennifer Pan, "How the Market for Social Media Shape Strategies of Internet Censorship," in *Digital Media and Democratic Futures*, ed. Michael X Delli Carpini (Philadelphia: University of Pennsylvania Press, 2019), 218.
29 Christopher Westland and Sherman So, *Red Wired: China's Internet Revolution* (London: Marshall Cavendish, 2010), 47.
30 Baidu, Annual report, 2005, 9, https://ir.baidu.com/static-files/7d4cade1-81b6-4a97-b92b-3948bd62d505.
31 "Baidu faces new suit on copyrights," *New York Times*, September 27, 2005, https://www.nytimes.com/2005/09/27/technology/baidu-faces-new-suit-on-copyrights.html.
32 Mike Masnick, "Yahoo China found guilty of copyright infringement for linking to MP3s," *Techdirt*, December 20, 2007, https://www.techdirt.com/2007/12/20/yahoo-china-found-guilty-of-copyright-infringement-for-linking-to-mp3s/.
33 Steven Schwankert, "Baidu beats labels in second court ruling," *Hollywood Reporter*, January 27, 2019, https://www.hollywoodreporter.com/business/business-news/baidu-beats-labels-second-court-19993/.
34 Xue "Snow" Dong and Krishna Jayakar, "The Baidu Music Settlement: A Turning Point for Copyright Reform In China?," *Journal of*

Information Policy, 3 (2013): 77-10,https://www.jstor.org/stable/10.5325/jinfopoli.3.2013.0077.

35 Eric Savitz, "Baidu hits U.S. list of "Notorious Markets" for infringing goods," *Forbes*, March 1, 2011, https://www.forbes.com/sites/ericsavitz/2011/03/01/baidu-hits-u-s-list-of-notorious-markets-for-infringing-goods/?sh=d3bfe104153e.

36 Dong Han, "How the Copyright Law Was (Not) Made: Intellectual Property and China's Contested Reintegration with Global Capitalism," *International Journal of Communication*, 8, no. 1 (2014): 1516–1535.

37 Dan Levin, "China's Biggest Search Engine, Known for Illegal Downloads, Makes Music Deal," *New York Times*, July 19, 2011, https://www.nytimes.com/2011/07/19/technology/baidu-chinas-search-giant-announces-music-licensing-deal.html.

38 Kai-Fu Lee, *AI Superpowers: China, Silicon Valley, and the New World Order* (Boston, MA: Houghton Mifflin Harcourt, 2019), 38.

39 Ibid.

40 Christopher Westland and Sherman So, *Red Wired: China's Internet Revolution* (London: Marshall Cavendish, 2010), 70.

41 Robin Wauters, "Baidu acquires dominant stake in online video firm iQiyi, buys out ex-Hulu investor Providence," *TNW*, November 2, 2012, http://thenextWeb.com/asia/2012/11/02/baidu-acquires-majority-stake-in-online-video-firm-iqiyi-buys-out-ex-hulu-investor-providence/.

42 Yunan Zhang and Juro Osawa, "Google's ad sales from China are booming," *The Information*, February 27, 2019, https://www.theinformation.com/articles/googles-ad-sales-from-china-are-booming.

43 Charles Arthur, "Microsoft strikes deal with China's biggest search engine Baidu," *Guardian*, July 4, 2011, https://www.theguardian.com/technology/2011/jul/04/microsoft-baidu-china-search-engines.

44 Lai Lin Thomala, "Market share of search engines in China 2021," *Statista*, January 14, 2022, https://www.statista.com/statistics/253340/market-share-of-search-engines-in-china-pageviews/.

45 "Chinese search engine market shares: Baidu – 52%, Google – 33%," *Zdnet*, August 30, 2005, https://www.zdnet.com/article/chinese-search-engine-market-shares-baidu-52-google-33/.

46 Loretta Chao, "Google loses Chinese market share," *Wall Street Journal*, April 27, 2010, https://www.wsj.com/articles/SB10001424052748703465204575207833281993688.

47 Paul Mozur, "Qihoo 360's Zhou Hongyi: Taking aim at China's internet," *Wall Street Journal*, November 30, 2012, http://online.wsj.com/article/SB10001424052970204707104578094460340552442.html.

48 Matt Marshall, "Yahoo China to file aggressive suit against Qihoo nemesis," *Venture Beat*, November 2, 2006, http://venturebeat.com/2006/11/03/yahoo-china-hits-back-at-qihoo-nemesis/.

49 Wenxian Zhang, Huiyao Wang, and Ilan Alon, *Entrepreneurial and Business Elites of China: The Chinese Returnees Who Have Shaped Modern China* (Bingley: Emerald Group Pub., 2011).

50 Alex Moazed and Nicholas L. Johnson, *Modern Monopolies What It Takes to Dominate the 21st-Century Economy* (New York: St. Martin's Press, 2016), 98.

51 Normandy Madden, "With Google gone, Baidu moves beyond search in China but faces local rivals," *Ad Age,* December 8, 2011, http://adage.com/article/global-news/baidu-moves-search-china-faces-local-rivals/231444/.
52 Zhang Ye, "Xinhua online portal files for IPO," *Global Times*, June 29, 2014, http://www.globaltimes.cn/content/868059.shtml.
53 Phill Muncaster, "Chinese government builds its own 'ChinaSo' search engine," *Register*, March 4, http://www.theregister.co.uk/2014/03/04/chinaso_search_engine_beijing_new/.
54 Min Jing, "Will China's new national search engine, ChinaSo, fare better than 'The Little Search Engine that Couldn't'?" *The Policy and Internet Blog*, February 10, 2015.
55 Lingling Wei, "Website of China communist party mouthpiece plans IPO," *Wall Street Journal*, January 10, 2012, http://online.wsj.com/article/SB10001424052970204124204577150563664941658.html.
56 "Search engine market share," *statcounter*, accessed October 14, 2020, https://gs.statcounter.com/search-engine-market-share/all/united-states-of-america.
57 Arjun Kharpal, "How China's tech trio – Baidu, Alibaba and Tencent – could fare in 2020," *CNBC*, January 20, 2020, https://www.cnbc.com/2020/01/10/china-tech-outlook-2020-baidu-bidu-alibaba-baba-and-tencent.html.
58 "ByteDance launches new search engine in China," *Reuters*, August 12, 2019, https://www.reuters.com/article/us-china-bytedance/bytedance-launches-new-search-engine-in-china-idUSKCN1V20Z7.
59 Ibid.
60 Yu Hong, *Networking China: The Digital Transformation of the Chinese Economy* (Champaign: University of Illinois Press, 2017); Min Tang, "From "bringing-in" to "going-out": Transnationalizing China's Internet Capital through State Policies," *Chinese Journal of Communication*, 13, no. 1 (2020): 27–46.

2 Economic Profile

Baidu is most well-known for its dominant search business; however, this chapter will show that the Chinese search giant is struggling in its core search business in the face of intense competition within both the domestic and international Internet markets, and therefore has an imperative to seek new market opportunities for its very survival. The chapter illustrates how Baidu has expanded and diversified its search engine business into artificial intelligence (AI)-driven industrial sectors including self-driving or autonomous cars (AVs), smart devices, cloud computing, etc. The company is in the midst of rebranding itself as an AI company, shifting from its original purpose of a consumer-oriented search engine company to an enterprise for the industrial Internet, attempting to make in-roads into new growth sectors and exploit China's new economic developmental path which is centered around innovation and upgrading China's industrial sectors. While the relationship between Baidu and politics will be discussed in the next chapter, Baidu's current and changing economic profile and accumulation strategies will set the stage to understanding the intersect between Baidu's business and China's changing political economy. By analyzing Baidu's myriad businesses, corporate structure, and financial profile, this chapter offers a window into the dynamics of the Internet market in China.

Struggling Search

Baidu is the largest search engine in China, dominating the search market across all platforms – desktop, mobile, and tablet. This command in search should secure Baidu's strong position over the Internet in China. Though Baidu's 2021 revenue was $19.536 billion, an increase over previous years, it significantly lagged behind its domestic competitors Tencent and Alibaba, respectively at $86.61

DOI: 10.4324/9781003189893-3

billion and $129.44 billion. Compared to Google's 2021 revenue of $256.7 billion, Baidu is still a small player in the global Internet market, controlling only a little over 1.6% of global search market share.[1] However, Baidu is clearly one of China's big three Internet companies, along with Chinese tech giants Tencent and Alibaba, that have occupied the key Internet domains – search, e-commerce, and video gaming – over the last two decades.

Baidu generates most of its revenues from advertising, a full two-thirds of its total revenue.[3] It relies on Chinese advertisers looking to reach China's burgeoning consumer market; it also depends on many foreign advertisers that utilize Baidu to tap into the growing overseas Chinese market. According to its 2020 annual report, Baidu stated that its competition was coming from both domestic and the US online marketing platforms including Tencent, Alibaba, Google, Facebook, and Microsoft Bing.[4] As mentioned earlier, Baidu is also competing against newer Chinese Internet companies like JD.com, ByteDance – owner Douyin which is known internationally as TikTok – and Meituan which are all chipping away at Baidu's core business generating advertising revenues (Figure 2.1).

Baidu's remaining revenue comes from its iQiyi streaming membership services, and its online marketing services and cloud unit. iQiyi is one of largest streaming platforms in China – along with Tencent video and Alibaba Youku – which will be discussed in more detail in Chapter 4 concerning Baidu's cultural profile. Baidu lists

	Year Ended December 31,					
	2017(1)	2018(2)	2019(2)	2020(2)	2021(2)	
	RMB	RMB	RMB	RMB	RMB	US$
	(In millions, except per share and per ADS data)					
Consolidated Statements of Comprehensive Income Data:						
Revenues:						
Online marketing services	73,146	81,912	78,093	72,840	80,695	12,663
Others	11,663	20,365	29,320	34,234	43,798	6,873
Total revenues	84,809	102,277	107,413	107,074	124,493	19,536
Operating costs and expenses:						
Cost of revenues	43,062	51,744	62,850	55,158	64,314	10,092
Selling, general and administrative	13,128	19,231	19,910	18,063	24,723	3,879
Research and development	12,928	15,772	18,346	19,513	24,938	3,914
Total operating costs and expenses	69,118	86,747	101,106	92,734	113,975	17,885
Operating profit	15,691	15,530	6,307	14,340	10,518	1,651
Total other income (loss), net	5,592	11,795	(6,647)	8,750	260	40
Income (loss) before income taxes	21,283	27,325	(340)	23,090	10,778	1,691
Income taxes	2,995	4,743	1,948	4,064	3,187	500
Net income (loss)	18,288	22,582	(2,288)	19,026	7,591	1,191
Less: Net loss attributable to non-controlling interests	(13)	(4,991)	(4,345)	(3,446)	(2,635)	(414)
Net income attributable to Baidu, Inc.	18,301	27,573	2,057	22,472	10,226	1,605

Figure 2.1 Baidu Income and Revenue Data
Source: Baidu, Annual Report, 2021.[2]

cloud under its other services, and generated almost $2.2 billion in revenue in 2021 (15.1 billion yuan) a growth of more than 25% from the previous year's revenue of $1.3 billion; though it is only approximately 10% of Baidu's total revenue, it should still be seen as one of Baidu's major growth sectors.[5] Baidu is diversifying its business in order to move away from solely relying on search ads revenue; however, until the company is able to create significant revenue from its other revenue sources, advertising is still important. China's digital ads market has been growing year over year. It reached approximately over $132 billion in 2021 and grew a 9.7% compared to the previous year.[6] However, Baidu's ads revenue has largely stagnated relative to its competitors and Baidu has fiercely fought to control and compete in the search market as seen by the company's pursuit of a series of legal actions against its competitors.

In 2019, Baidu sued ByteDance's Toutiao search for unfair competition and claimed ByteDance was redirecting Baidu users' search results to ByteDance content.[7] Previously, Baidu had previously filed a lawsuit against ByteDance for stealing its search results, defamation, and copyright infringement for stealing AI technology.[8] In response, ByteDance sued Baidu for copying its short videos clips.[9] The cutthroat inter-capitalist competition has driven the tech companies to do anything to stymie their competitors including blocking them from indexing content.

The value of a search engine is to provide access to a growing pool of fresh, publicly available information. However, Baidu's competitors like WeChat, ByteDance, JD.com, and Meituan have all created "walled garden" supper apps that block Baidu from indexing, pulling in and combining different kinds of third-party services, news, messaging, shopping, and entertainment and with algorithmic feeding and search functions of their own. With an increasing amount of content being private and not accessible, the value of Baidu's search engine function has been diminishing and struggling to draw web traffic.

Baidu's desperation to maintain its search ads business once manifested in a public outcry over its deteriorating search quality. Fang Kecheng, then a PhD candidate at the Annenberg School for Communication at the University of Pennsylvania and currently an assistant professor at Chinese University of Hong Kong, wrote a scathing criticism on Weibo titled "Baidu is Dead."[10] He pointed out that the company was directing its search results to its own content publishing platforms like Baijiahao and Baidu Baike.[11] While Baidu refuted Kecheng's claim, the public outcry was enough that the company said they would improve their search quality.[12] Baidu's future growth in online advertising remains far from certain considering an array of available platforms and depressed online ads prices.[13]

With the intense competition in the domestic Internet market, Baidu had long searched for new international markets to expand. In 2007, Baidu first launched its Japanese services, partnering with Japanese e-commerce giant Rakuten; yet its global expansion hasn't been a smooth road.[14] At that time in Japan, Yahoo! dominated the market with over 50% market share – although Yahoo! search in Japan was powered by the Google search algorithm and Google also controlled over 36% of the Japanese market.[15] Microsoft had even attempted to convince Yahoo! Japan to use Bing's search algorithm, but this effort failed because SoftBank, the Japanese cellphone maker and Yahoo! Japan's major stakeholder, refused their overture because of the larger benefit of using Google search technology strength in Japanese language queries.[16] As a newcomer, Baidu was dealing with incumbents Yahoo! and Google, and was not able to make a dent in the Japanese search market. Baidu barely got 1% of the market share, and in the end, the company closed its Japanese search business in 2015.[17]

Despite its unsuccessful venture in Japan, Baidu expanded its various services, targeting countries in Southeast Asia, South America, and the Middle East including Vietnam, Thailand, Indonesia, India, Brazil, and Egypt, partnering with local and multinational tech companies.[18] Baidu focused on the emerging markets and/or non-English territories strategically because there was space for growth in areas not yet fully occupied by Google and other US firms. Baidu also had its eye on Google's home turf, the US and Europe. Baidu expanded its mapping services, working with tourist administrations of Denmark, Finland, Norway, and Sweden to target China's outbound tourism market, thus directly competing with Google map and Apple map.[19] However, Baidu's first 10 years of "going out" operations and major investments have been largely unsuccessful. Thus, its business is still almost exclusively within China as Baidu continues to struggle to expand into international markets. With increasing tension between the US and China, Baidu's search venture into the global market is far from promising and its domestic market has become more important than ever. With a fiercely competitive domestic market and failure in its international ventures, Baidu has looked to raise additional capital to offset its international losses and cultivate new domestic growth markets. Baidu's corporate structure was set up in a way to tap into global capital markets.

Corporate Structure and Properties

Baidu Inc. was incorporated in the Cayman Islands using the Variable Interest Entity (VIE) structure. As stated in an earlier chapter, the VIE structure allows foreign investors to invest in and have a claim on a Chinese operation's profits and assets through contractual agreements with the VIE rather than through a legal obligation. This arrangement facilitates mutual interests between Chinese companies and foreign capital as it allows Chinese firms access to global capital and foreign capital access to lucrative Chinese Internet firms. The VIE structure has facilitated Baidu's integration into the global financial market as well as financialization of Chinese Internet sector (Figure 2.2).

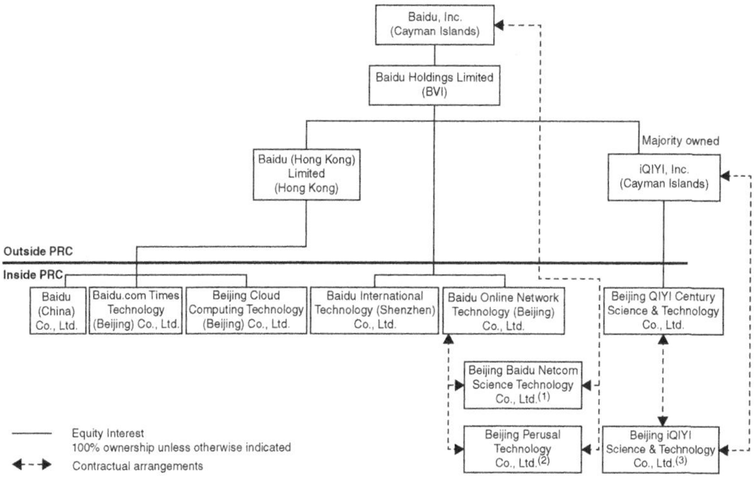

Figure 2.2 Baidu Corporate Structure
Source: Baidu 2021 Form 6-K.[20]

However, because of the escalating tensions between China and the US, China was pressured to deal with the VIE structure. In the past, there was an attempt by the People's Republic of China (PRC) to regulate the VIE structure, but the state had never acted upon that pressure. However, in 2021, the China Securities Regulatory Commission (CSRC) announced that it would revise the VIE legal framework and require approval from the state filing with the CSRC.[21] Interestingly, the new legal framework didn't ban VIEs outright nor was it intended to affect companies currently under the VIE structure. Rather it gave support for China's continued opening up and allowed companies to be listed overseas 20 days after filing with the CSRC.[22] By implementing the regulatory framework, the PRC legitimized its ability to intervene as needed but at the same time did not shut off Chinese companies' access to the large pool of capital from the US-based capital markets for start-ups.

The PRC's shift in VIE policy was spurred by the Trump Administration's push to exercise power over Chinese tech companies. In 2020, the US Congress passed a law called the Holding Foreign Companies Accountable Act (HFCAA) which required that the US Securities and Exchange Commission (SEC) regulate and audit public companies with offices in foreign jurisdictions.[23] Under HFCAA, Chinese companies listed on the US stock exchange would be required to be audited and disclose their state ownership, and the SEC could delist any Chinese companies from the US exchange if those companies failed to comply with US auditing standards.[24] HFCAA was meant to target 254 Chinese companies listed on the US stock exchange for possible delisting including Baidu and Alibaba.[25] The PRC understood the cost to Chinese companies of being delisted from the US stock exchange as they would be cut off from the US capital markets. The Chinese state encouraged Chinese Internet companies to cooperate with the US, removed barriers for US regulators, and offered the SEC access to the CSRC's auditing reports of Chinese companies.[26] Through doing so, the Chinese Communist Party (CCP) signaled the ongoing importance for Chinese tech companies' ability to plug into the US capital market.

In May 2020, Baidu CEO Robin Li said in an interview: "we are indeed very concerned about the continuous tightening of this kind of control on Chinese stocks from the government level in the United States."[27] This geopolitical tension has prompted Baidu to list the company secondarily on the Hong Kong Stock Exchange, which raised $3.1 billion.[28] The second listing allowed Baidu not only to raise additional capital but also to diversify its shareholder base which reduced risk. And the additional funds raised, helped commercialize the company's new businesses – AVs, electric appliances, cloud computing, and AI chips. Baidu is just one of the Chinese tech companies which have second listed in Hong Kong. The major Chinese Internet companies Alibaba, Tencent Netease, JD.com, and Bilibili are all now second listed in Hong Kong.

Pivot to AI

As Baidu has continued to struggle in its core search business, the company has looked for new strategies to turn around its business. For years, the company invested in various adjacent online services; however, Baidu has failed so far to sustain its businesses into those areas. Since 2013, Baidu has gradually begun to reorient its business to AI, investing significant amounts of capital[29] and filing for more than 9000 AI-related patents in China.[30]

Today, Baidu is trying to leverage its AI technology to regain its market power across major growth sectors – AI-driven mobile platform, Internet of Things (IoT) devices, cloud, autonomous vehicles (AVs), and electric vehicles (EVs). Baidu has enormous amounts of search data accumulated over several decades, but search data are not necessarily helpful for all of Baidu's new AI sectors. Baidu has therefore taken a page from Google's playbook. As Google deployed its open-source android operating system to compete against Apple, Baidu has also taken the open-source accumulation strategy to diffuse its AI operating system as widely as possible, attract application developers, collect data, and penetrate a range of different markets.[31] Baidu's open-source AI platform called "Baidu Brain" is embedded in various platforms – deep learning platform *Paddle Paddle*, voice search platform *DUerOS*, and *Apollo* for AVs. Baidu is also seeking to collaborate with a wide variety of domestic and foreign hardware manufacturing companies and looking for ways to extend its network.

Baidu's voice search platform DUerOS is key to Baidu's strategy to regain search dominance and a core part of its IoT strategy. DUerOS, which supports various appliances, powers both Baidu-built and third-party devices. In 2018, Baidu established a separate unit called the *Smart Living Group (SLG)* with its voice assistant at its core to inject new capital. SLG raised $3 billion from Citic Private Equity, Baidu's investment capital arm Baidu Capital, and IDG Capital. Baidu's SLG aims for the growing global smart home market which is expected to reach over $126 billion by 2022 and encompasses home appliances, home entertainment, security, lighting, etc.[32] Baidu is competing domestically against Alibaba and Xiaomi which are leading the smart home sector and globally with Apple, Google, Amazon, and Samsung. At the same time, these companies are allying to establish interoperability standards for the smart home market which has been limited by the lack of standards.[33]

Baidu has a range of smart devices under its Xiaodu voice assistant brand including speakers, televisions, wireless earphones, refrigerators, computer mice, and other electronic appliances all enabled with its AI voice assistant. Xiaodu had completed a $5.1 billion valuation in 2020.[34]

In 2018, Baidu's smart speakers held less than 1% market share, but Baidu's tactic was to sell their speakers at half price to gain a greater market share against Baidu's domestic competitor Alibaba and Xiaomi, both of which also cut their prices.[35] By 2019, Baidu had become the largest Chinese smart speaker manufacturer, selling 13 million smart speakers with a growth rate of almost 280%.[36] Baidu become the third largest global vender of smart speakers with a market share of 13.6%, trailing only behind Amazon's echo at 25.5% and Google Home with 20.5%.[37] The reason for this price war was not only to squeeze out competitors and start-ups but also to win the race to build a large user base for first move advantage considering the smart speaker market was a new segment of the market. After gaining a significant market share and being a major player, Baidu terminated its subsidy for smart speakers.

To capture IoT, Baidu is also building out strategic partnerships with a slew of hardware companies. The company is working with Midea, one of China's biggest home appliance manufacturers, which produces all kinds of products from rice cookers to heaters to air conditioners, microwave ovens, and lights. AI-powered smart home devices are clearly core pieces of Baidu's artificial intelligence (AI) unit and critical to its capital expansion strategy. Baidu's IoT business, which generates vast amounts of data, is built on its own AI cloud infrastructure that has turned into an extremely lucrative business.

AI Cloud

Baidu is beefing up its cloud business as a long-term strategy. It has launched Baidu Intelligent Cloud which consists of AI, big data, and cloud computing (ABC). The three clusters of Baidu's AI cloud platform are smart multimedia cloud *TianXiang*, which offers facial recognition, live video streaming and image processing service, big data platform *TianSuan*, and IoT platform *TianGong* used by the energy, automobile, and logistics sectors. As noted earlier, the combination of AI with a cloud computing environment is rapidly becoming one of Baidu's core businesses. This is still only a small portion of the company's overall revenue of $19.54 billion in 2021, but it's the fastest growing sector for Baidu.[38]

Considering that AI hinges on data and computing power, cloud infrastructure has become vital for both Baidu's internal data and storage and computing use as well as for its new AI profit sector. With China's growth of its digital economy, the cloud infrastructure service market has been boosted and reached $6.6 billion in 2020, the second largest in the world behind the US.[39] This is still a fraction of the US cloud market which reached over $140 billion in 2022,[40] but the market is growing rapidly as the Chinese government's new digital infrastructure initiatives – smart cities, smart transportation, and industrial Internet – are accelerating the growth of China's domestic cloud market. Baidu wants to seize this bourgeoning market. In China, Baidu, Alibaba, Huawei, and Tencent hold a combined 80% of the domestic cloud market.[41] Baidu holds 9% of the cloud market, while the other big tech companies are leading the sector. Alibaba has 37% of the market, Huawei has 18% and Tencent has 16%. But Baidu made a big push in the sector and was leading in terms of growth rate with over 64 % in the last quarter of 2021.[42] In search of growth, Baidu has also rebooted its global market expansion by opening up a cloud service in Singapore – where domestic competitors Alibaba, Tencent, Amazon, and Huawei as well as the US rivals Google, Amazon, and Microsoft are all already operating – and aiming to expand across southeast Asia.

Still, Baidu is facing an uphill battle in the cloud market. To make up ground on the other companies, Baidu is seeking to partner with local governments and industrial enterprises as provincial governments in China compete against each other to implement new technologies in response to national economic developments and "smart city" initiatives. As China is planning to restructure its manufacturing sector with the implementation of advanced information technologies – cloud, 5G, and IoT – to be more competitive in the global value chain,[43] Baidu is attempting to capitalize on its cloud business in China's industrial sectors – manufacturing, healthcare, and transportation – as the company seeks to profit by deeply interconnecting to the Chinese state's economic development plans. One example of this is the company's joint venture with the Shunde District Government of Foshan City, Guangdong Province. The company has established its cloud computing center to enhance the city's traditional manufacturing industry.[44] The company's AI cloud was awarded a $27.7 million project to work with the provincial government in Tongxiang, Zhejiang province to create advanced manufacturing clusters built on its industrial Internet platform.[45] Baidu also signed on to work with China Gas Holdings Limited as part of building "smart cities" by deploying a range of applications into the energy sector.

By taking advantage of its AI-powered cloud infrastructure, Baidu has also entered the connected transportation market which is driving the restructuring and upgrading of China's existing automobile industry with the introduction of digital technologies.

Automobile Industry

Baidu's most critical, ambitious, and invested AI business is the transportation sector. The global AVs market is expected to reach over $37 billion by 2023.[46] In the US, Google's Waymo – formerly the Google Self-driving Car Project – and GM's Cruise are leading the pack with increasing consolidation, but in China, Baidu is leading and poised to challenge its US competitors for dominance of the global market. In 2017, the company released its AI-powered open-source AV platform *Apollo* and allowed anyone to download and use the software. By exploiting open-source software development, the company is positioning itself at the center of future data flows. Baidu's aim is to make Apollo the "Android for AVs" to empower a wide variety of vehicles.

Baidu controls its open source Apollo OS platform to power AVs. The platform is comprised of complex software and hardware architecture including core software, cloud, GPS, camera, lidar, etc. There is no one company to source all of the components of the platform as the software has over 700,000 lines of source code, and 80,000+ developers around the world.[47] Deploying its own AI technologies, Baidu began to test its AVs on the road starting in 2015. Enabled by local city governments which gave the company the green light to test vehicles, Baidu took its AVs across 13 cities including Beijing and Shanghai and also built its own self-driving test facility in Chongqing in collaboration with the local government.[48] As of 2020, Baidu owned a total of 55 licensed self-driving testing vehicles in China.[49]

In the international market, Baidu is one of six AV companies to receive permission from the California State Department of Motor

Vehicles to test a fully autonomous car without a human driver behind the wheel.[50] The others include Cruise, Waymo, Nuro, Amazon's Zoox, and AutoX, a startup funded by Alibaba.

Baidu has assembled over 200 global industry partnerships. These include Chinese auto firms, as well as foreign companies, such as Daimler, Volkswagen, Ford, and Toyota,[51] US chip companies Intel and Nvidia for AI hardware and software, Dutch company TomTom for map data, German auto suppliers Robert Bosch and Continental AG, BlackBerry for high-definition real time map operating system, and Microsoft's cloud for cloud services outside China.[52] Rather than "decoupling," Baidu's corporate strategy is clearly to integrate its OS into the global AV value chain.

Baidu has extended its AV business to multimode vehicles – taxis, shuttles, and buses.[53] In 2018, Baidu and state-owned carmaker FAW Group announced that they would produce a level 4 self-driving car – these cars do not require human interaction for the most part[54] – to deploy in Hunan's capital of Changsha. In 2020, Changsha served as a test site for Baidu's robot taxi project. Baidu was also awarded a $67 million smart transportation project in conjunction with Guangzhou-based Sci Group and Guangzhou Public Transport Group.[55] As part of the project to build an intelligent transport network in the city, Baidu constructed an infrastructure to operate robotaxis and 5G-powered robo buses for public transportation.[56] Baidu already operates a paid driverless taxi service in Beijing's Shougang Park – which was previously an industrial iron and steel factory but was developed to host the Beijing 2020 Winter Olympics. The company aims to run 3000 fully driverless Apollo Go Robotaxis in 30 cities by 2023.[57]

Baidu is also extending its automobile business into electric vehicles (EVs) and moving beyond the development of software to manufacturing EVs through a strategic partnership. In early 2021, Baidu set up a new joint EV car company *Jiju Auto* with private Chinese automaker Geely which merged with Swedish automaker Volvo to manufacture EVs.[58] The company owns the majority of this new unit.[59] *Jiju Auto* is currently raising capital with plans to develop a robot EV in 2023.

Baidu made early moves in the EV sector, but it is not the only player. Baidu's domestic and foreign tech competitors have all joined the race in the booming EV sector including Didi, Xiaomi, Huawei, Alibaba, state-owned automaker SAIC Motor, Tencent-backed Nio, Xpeng Li Auto, BMV, Warren Buffett-backed BYD, Tesla, and GM-backed Momenta. China's EV market is quickly heating up as more than 300 licensed carmakers are competing with each other.[60] One of the reasons for the crowded EV market is because since 2010, the PRC has been promoting the EV industry and stimulating the entire sector by offering tax breaks, building out public infrastructure, and subsidizing consumers' purchase of EV cars to spur competition.[61] Between 2009 and 2021, the Chinese government subsidized EVs to the tune of $14.8 billion and is set to extend their support until 2023.[62] For the last few years, China has also been developing domestic EV component suppliers in order to lower the cost of production and control the market.[63] In fact, China dominates Lithium-Ion Battery manufacturing for EVs. China was the world's biggest market for EVs, selling 1.3 million vehicles in 2020 which accounted for 40% of sales worldwide.[64] The country built more than 1.15 million public electric vehicle charging stations[65] compared to 113,600 charging outlets in the US as of 2022.[66] Baidu is gearing up to be a major player in this sector.

To be competitive across the array of its industrial AI businesses, Baidu is taking up the manufacture of AI chips, a new type of chip with the speed, efficiency and power required of AI. Baidu relies on US chip suppliers for its general-purpose chips. However, the company has recognized the importance of the AI chip which functions as a brain of AI applications. In addition, since the semiconductor industry is dominated by the US and its ally Taiwan, there is a danger for Baidu to being cut off from the global chip supply chain with the ongoing geopolitical conflict. Thus, Baidu, wanting to control the entire value chain, began manufacturing its own AI chip.

AI Chips

With the growth of AI applications, Baidu has been investing in the booming AI chip market which is expected to reach $70.9 billion by 2026 with a compound annual growth rate (CAGR) of approximately 42.3%.[67] The AI chip is vital to controlling performance and integration of software and hardware and in supporting various AI applications such as image recognition, autonomous driving, voice recognition, search ranking, deep learning algorithms, and data transfers. In 2021, Baidu created an independent chip unit *Kunlun* – which completed a round of fundraising and was valued at $2 billion – and began to mass produce its second-generation *Kunlun* AI chips.

Baidu's AI chips are deployed internally in its data center, public cloud, and AVs to maximize AI processing. In addition to internal use, it is also looking to its chip unit to be a core business as China's insatiable demand for computer chips continues to grow on top of the PRC's push to develop its domestic semiconductor industry to alleviate the country's reliance on foreign suppliers. China has bet on AI chips rather than pursuing traditional chips like memory chips and mobile processors because US, Taiwanese, and South Korean firms control the entire production chain (not to mention the patents) of traditional chip production.[68] This is one of China's choke points in the supply chain as chips are vital for computer power and electronic devices. In 2020, the US Commerce Department even put Chinese chipmaker Semiconductor Manufacturing International Corp (SMIC) on its "entity list," blocking SMIC's access to critical technologies from US suppliers.[69] Interestingly, despite SMIC being on the US trade blacklist, the company has been able to access the US technologies as the US government has granted the export licenses which are worth $61 billion to the US suppliers.[70] The US has sought to assert its power over the supply chain to undercut China; however, the deep-rooted interdependence limits US maneuverability.

By focusing on AI chips, China's strategy is to control the bottlenecks and reduce reliance on imported integrated circuits amid growing tensions with the US. China's Internet sector is rushing into the AI chip business to power new technologies across sectors. Baidu's domestic competitors Alibaba, Tencent, Huawei, and Metiuan, with Chinese state-backing, have all entered the AI chip-making sector.[71] As these Chinese tech giants have begun to design and produce their own AI chips, they are challenging the US chip companies like Nvidia which dominate the rapidly-growing AI chip market.[72] Despite US restrictions on exports to Chinese chipmakers, the Chinese chip sector has attracted almost $11 billion in foreign – and US – venture capital in 2021.[73] In particular, major chip companies including Intel and private investors are pouring capital into China's semiconductor companies.[74]

Within this context, Baidu's chip business is important not simply to reduce costs and increase performance across its AI concerns; it is also part of its own growth sector as well as critical within the conflict between China and the US which has driven Chinese tech companies to produce their own chips in order to create leverage against the US chipmakers.[75] However, it's also worth noting that the manufacturing of their own AI chips is not unique to Baidu or uncommon among the global tech companies. Google, Amazon, Facebook, and many other tech companies are now all developing their own AI chips to be more competitive by improving performance, power, and efficiency within their internal infrastructures.

Peripheries

David Harvey notes that in capitalism, once a technology becomes a business, it needs to search for and create new markets to sell the technology.[76] Deploying its AI technologies, Baidu has extended its business into other economic sectors and in particular, into health and finance. These sectors are not Baidu's core per se at this point, but they are crucial for the company's growth considering they are rapidly being digitized, with booming businesses promoted by the state. In 2015, Baidu's AI Innovation Unit began to work in the medical AI sector, investing in an AI-powered chatbot for medical consultations.[77] Boosted by the Covid pandemic, Baidu has accelerated the introduction of a range of AI-driven healthcare diagnostic tools,[78] and is now operating an online medical consultation platform with 100,000 doctors.[79] Baidu is also exploring the launch of a separate biotech startup and speculating for possible investors.

Meanwhile its competitors are marching into the sector: Alibaba Health sells medical services, medical consultation services, and health screening; Tencent's medical unit has created a private healthcare network offering on- and offline services; Huawei is involved in drug deliveries and online medial consultations; JD.com is building its own on- and offline health business including pharmaceutical products and an Internet hospital.[80] The Chinese state has been backing the development of the health tech industry and has sped up the process due to the pandemic as the state now promotes Internet-based medical services as part of pushing its Internet Plus Healthcare (IPHC) – a model that integrates and applies information technologies including mobile Internet, cloud computing, big data, and AI.[81]

Besides the health sector, Baidu has long been a player in the financial technology (fintech) sector which includes mobile payments, digital banking, insurance, wealth management, cryptocurrency, and cross-border payment. The sector has gotten much attention after Alibaba's fintech arm Ant Group's initial IPO in November 2020 on the Shanghai and Hong Kong stock exchanges was suspended by the CCP for its anti-competitive behavior, but the Chinese fintech industry has been leading the global market. In 2005, Baidu launched its fintech arm "Baidu Finance" and sought to compete against its rivals Alibaba and Tencent. While Baidu Finance never quite took off, China's fintech sector led by Alibaba, Tencent, Ping An, and JD.com quickly outpaced the US and began reshaping the financial market. By 2018, China ranked first in fintech investments reaching $25.5 billion, which accounted for 46% of global fintech investment.[82] The industry's growth also drew attention from the regulators as the non-financial industry had begun operating in the traditional financial market. There were several attempts by the CCP to regulate the sector, but the party state tolerated this to avoid any disturbances of the financial system. This favorable relaxed environment fostered a drastic growth of the fintech companies as well as the systemic financial risk of capital outflow from traditional banks.[83]

However, Baidu was lagging behind the duopoly of the Ant Group and WeChat Pay, the dominant players in the sector. Thus, in 2019, Baidu restructured its fintech unit, sold off the major part of its financial services and renamed it Du Xiaoman Financial, raising capital from US private-equity giants TPG and the Carlyle Group, and the Agricultural Bank of China.[84] The company is more focused on providing technical solutions for banks and financial institutions, selling its data analysis service and computing power by utilizing the company's AI technology and technical infrastructure.[85]

After the CCP stepped in to suspend Ant Group's IPO, which cost the company nearly $60 billion, Baidu's fintech efforts also faltered momentarily. The regulators' strike against Ant Group could be perceived as the CCP's attempt to curtail the private fintech sector which was encroaching on the territory of the state-backed traditional banks. However, the CCP's move was not meant to undermine the development of the private fintech sector; rather it was intended to strike a balance between fintech development and the mitigation of evolving financial risk posed by Internet companies. In fact, the fintech sector is one of the target industries for the CCP to be developed as AI- and blockchain technologies are encouraged to be implemented. Recently, the party state has been tightening up the fintech market, requiring licenses, creating a wall between insurance and wealth management and direct links between non-bank and banking services.[86] The People's Bank of China (PBOC) released its Fintech Development Plan for 2022–2025, calling for the development of China's fintech sector and the digitization of its financial sector within the next few years.[87] The plan is part of China's 14th Five Year Plan (FYP) and supports measures to develop the fintech market – including implementing new rules and regulations, strengthening security and privacy, and building a platform to connect business, technology, and data, etc.[88]

In response, Baidu signaled a reset of its own fintech business and introduced a blockchain service "Open Network" based on Baidu's open-source blockchain protocol *XuperChain*. Baidu partnered with several institutions – including the Beijing Internet Court, Peking University, electric vehicle giant TGOOD, AiBank, etc. – to host its Xuperchain nodes.[89] The service provides an open-source blockchain as a service, enabling users a "plug and play" platform to develop and deploy applications without building their own blockchain platforms. Baidu is clearly gearing up to capitalize on the financial sector.

Conclusion

This chapter examined Baidu's economic profile. Unlike the mainstream rhetoric of a Chinese market tightly controlled by the state, Baidu's business shows an extremely competitive and dynamic Chinese Internet market imbued with both domestic and transnational capital. Baidu is dominant in search, but its core ads business has eroded over the years because of intense competition within both the domestic and international markets. Domestically, Baidu had to cultivate a new growth sector beyond search, while internationally had to withdraw some of its businesses. To be a viable company, Baidu had to reorganize its business and move away from its ads-centered search to restore its profit base. Baidu is still relying on its search ads business, but its core ads business is subsidizing Baidu's new growth sectors – the company has transformed itself into an AI company. Deploying an open-source strategy, Baidu has inserted its Apollo AV operating system into the entire value chain through collaborations with domestic as well as US and global companies. To facilitate Baidu's growth sector, Baidu's corporate structure still relies on VIEs which is firmly embedded in the global financial market.

Baidu is repositioning itself as an AI company, but its growth is not just relying on its technical innovations; rather it hinges more on China's changing political economy. In particular, the expansion of Baidu's industrial AI businesses including AVs and EVs require public infrastructure, urban planning, and new regulatory environments. The next chapter will show how Baidu's business is tightly interconnected with China's new industrial policy. The PRC has motivated the private Internet giants to move up the economic value chain as it dances between market dynamics, interests of national development, and the new geopolitical landscape.

Notes

1 Joseph Johnson, "Baidu's search engine market share worldwide 2018–2021," *Statista*, October 14, 2021, https://www.statista.com/statistics/1219413/market-share-held-by-baidu-worldwide/.
2 Baidu, Annual Report, 2021, 8, https://ir.baidu.com/financial-reports.
3 Lai Lin Thomala, "Baidu's annual revenue sources 2021," *Statista*, April1,2022,https://www.statista.com/statistics/1106208/baidu-annual-revenue-by-product/.
4 Baidu, Annual Report, 2020, 80. https://ir.baidu.com/financial-reports
5 Lai Lin Thomala, "Annual revenue of Baidu's cloud services from 2018 to 2021," *Statista,* April 1, 2022, https://www.statista.com/statistics/1232271/cloud-services-revenue-of-baidu/.
6 Lai Lin Thomala, "Revenue of the online advertising industry in China from 2013 to 2020 with a forecast until 202," *Statista*, December 22, 2021, https://www.statista.com/statistics/796017/china-online-advertising-revenue/.
7 Ding Yi, "Baidu escalates legal battle with Bytedance over search results," *Caixing Global*, December 20, 2019, https://www.caixinglobal.com/2019-12-20/baidu-escalates-legal-battle-with-bytedance-over-search-results-101496236.html.
8 Wei Seng, "Bytedance responds to Baidu's accusations of manipulating search results," *technode*, December 30, 2019, https://technode.com/2019/12/30/bytedances-search-engine-accused-of-meddling-with-results-by-baidu-company-counters/.
9 Jill Shen, "In a series of three firsts, Beijing's internet court dismisses ByteDance copyright suit against Baidu," *technode*, December 27, 2018, https://technode.com/2018/12/27/chinas-first-short-video-lawsuit/.
10 Echo Huang, "An obituary for Baidu argues China's vast internet has no search engine," *Quartz*, January 24, 2019, https://qz.com/1530831/an-obituary-for-baidu-argues-chinas-vast-internet-has-no-search-engine/.
11 Ibid.
12 Josh Horwitz, "China's Baidu pledges to improve search service after complaint," *Reuters*, January 23, 2019, https://www.reuters.com/article/us-china-tech-baidu/chinas-baidu-pledges-to-improve-search-service-after-complaint-idUSKCN1PH0M3.
13 "Baidu turns to personal transport for growth," *The Economist*, March 18, 2021.
14 Hiroko Tabuchi, "Yahoo Japan teams with Google on search," *New York Times*, July 27, 2010, http://www.nytimes.com/2010/07/28/technology/28yahoo.html?_r=0.
15 Kenj Schaulzer, "Japan search engine market share 2013," *Search Blog Asia*, February 15, 2012, http://www.searchblog.asia/topics/seo/japan-search-engine-market-share-2012/.
16 Hiroko Tabuchi, "Yahoo Japan teams with Google on search," *New York Times*, July 27, 2010, http://www.nytimes.com/2010/07/28/technology/28yahoo.html?_r=0.
17 Cyrus Lee, "Baidu leaves Japanese search market," *ZDNet,* April 20, 2015, https://www.zdnet.com/article/baidu-leaves-japanese-search-market/.

18 Nicole Lee, "Baidu and Orange launch mobile browser for Africa, Middle East," *Engadget*, January 15, 2013, https://www.engadget.com/2013-01-15-baidu-orange-browser-africa-middle-east.html.
19 "Baidu maps out global expansion," *China Daily*, November 29, 2016, http://www.china.org.cn/business/2016-11/29/content_39808098.htm.
20 Baidu, "Baidu Annual Report," United States Securities and Exchange Commission (SEC) Form 6-K, March 2021, https://ir.baidu.com/node/12416/html.
21 Jeremy Goldkorn, "Did China take another step to financial decoupling with new VIE rules?" *SupChina*, July 7, 2021, https://supchina.com/2021/07/07/did-china-take-another-step-to-financial-decoupling-with-new-vie-rules/.
22 Brendan Ahern, "CSRC confirms support for VIE structure," *Forbes*, December 27, 2021, https://www.forbes.com/sites/brendanahern/2021/12/27/csrc-confirms-support-for-vie-structure/?sh=12b0cfc1235c.
23 US Securities and Exchange Commission, "Holding Foreign Companies Accountable Act ("HFCAA")," August 29, 2022, https://www.sec.gov/hfcaa.
24 "SEC starts the clock on audit-linked Chinese stock delistings," *Asia Financial*, March 24, 2021, https://www.asiafinancial.com/sec-starts-the-clock-on-audit-linked-chinese-stock-delistings.
25 Ben Bain, Naoreen Chowdhury and Michael Smallberg, "How the US is moving closer to delisting Chinese firms," *Washington Post*, April 2, 2022, https://www.washingtonpost.com/business/how-the-us-is-moving-closer-to-delisting-chinese-firms/2022/04/03/b69c5ef0-b3bb-11ec-8358-20aa16355fb4_story.html.
26 "China removes key hurdle to allow US full access to audits," *Bloomberg*, April 2, 2022, https://www.bloomberg.com/news/articles/2022-04-02/china-removes-major-hurdle-to-allow-u-s-full-access-to-audits.
27 Palash Ghosh, "Will Chinese stocks delist from US exchanges under increasing pressure from Washington?," *International Business Times*, May 22, 2020, https://www.ibtimes.com/will-chinese-stocks-delist-us-exchanges-under-increasing-pressure-washington-2981036?ft=739nr&utm_source=GoogleNewsstandBusiness&utm_medium=Feed&utm_campaign=_content.
28 Scott Murdoch, "China's Baidu raises $3.1 billion from Hong Kong listing," *Reuters*, March 17, 2012, https://www.reuters.com/article/us-baidu-listing/chinas-baidu-raises-3-1-billion-from-hong-kong-listing-idUSKBN2B90H2.
29 Yuan Yang and Yingzhi Yang, "Baidu bets its future on AI revolution," *Financial Times*, August 29, 2017, https://www.ft.com/content/3bd8dc72-7c0a-11e7-9108-edda0bcbc928.
30 "Baidu holds the most AI-related patents in China," China Internet Watch, December 7, 2020, https://www.chinainternetwatch.com/31482/baidu-ai-patents/.
31 Emily Feng and Yuan Yang, "Baidu offers open-source car software as lure for data," *Financial Times*, July 5, 2017, https://www-ft-com.stanford.idm.oclc.org/content/55e79944-6168-11e7-91a7-502f7ee26895.
32 Statista Research Department, "Smart home," *Statista*, March 16, 2022, https://www.statista.com/outlook/dmo/smart-home/worldwide.

33 Jennifer Pattison Tuohy, "Matter's plan to save the smart home," *Verge*, December 28, 2021, https://www.theverge.com/22787729/matter-smart-home-standard-apple-amazon-google.
34 "Baidu's AI voice assistant Xiaodu closes funding at $5.1 bln valuation," *Reuters*, August 24, 2021, https://www.reuters.com/technology/baidus-ai-voice-assistant-xiaodu-closes-funding-51-bln-valuation-2021-08-24/.
35 Cyrus Lee, "Baidu ends huge subsidies on smart speakers amid price wars in China," *ZDNet*, December 19, 2019, https://www.zdnet.com/article/baidu-ends-huge-subsidies-on-smart-speakers-amid-price-wars-in-china/.
36 Daniel Slota, "Quarterly growth rate of smart speaker shipments in China in 4th quarter 2019, by brand," *Statista*, September 21, 2021, https://www.statista.com/statistics/945017/china-growth-rate-of-smart-speaker-shipments-by-brand/.
37 Federica Lariccha, "Global smart speaker market share 2016–2021, by vendor," *Statista*, March 22, 2022, https://www.statista.com/statistics/792604/worldwide-smart-speaker-market-share/.
38 Lai Lin Thomala, "Annual revenue of Baidu from 2011 to 2021," *Statista*, June 16, 2022, https://www-statista-com.stanford.idm.oclc.org/statistics/269032/annual-revenue-of-baidu/.
39 Alice Kantor, "Cloud becomes new front line between China and the West," *Financial Times*, May 17, 2021, https://www.ft.com/content/ddc4d6ff-13dc-449d-a4ca-9ad3d1d6a184.
40 "Public Cloud," *Statista*, https://www.statista.com/outlook/tmo/public-cloud/united-states#revenue.
41 "China cloud computing market in 2021; top 4 have 80% market share," China Internet Watch, Aril 2, 2022, https://www.chinainternetwatch.com/30820/cloud-infrastructure-services/.
42 Iris Deng, "Huawei, Tencent lose cloud market share as Alibaba, Baidu extend their lead, report shows," *South China Morning Post*, December 13, 2021, https://www.scmp.com/tech/tech-trends/article/3159483/huawei-tencent-lose-cloud-market-share-alibaba-baidu-extend-their.
43 Greg Ip, "China wants manufacturing – not the internet – to lead the economy," *Wall Street Journal*, August 4, 2021, https://www.wsj.com/articles/china-wants-manufacturingnot-the-internetto-lead-the-economy-11628078155.
44 "Baidu '10-Billion-Yuan Project' settled in Shunde Park of Foshan High-tech Zone," Foshan National Hi-tech Industrial Development Zone, September 3, 2020, http://fs-hitech.foshan.gov.cn/en/en/investment/content/post_4626962.html.
45 Fan Feifei, "Cloud infrastructure market sees rapid expansion," *China Daily*, September 23, 2021, https://inf.news/en/tech/3c78efe659395a44d-f1b30670c02717a.html.
46 Martin Placek, "Size of the global autonomous car market from 2019 to 2023," *Statista*, June 22, 2012, https://www.statista.com/statistics/428692/projected-size-of-global-autonomous-vehicle-market-by-vehicle-type/.
47 Egil Juliussen, "How Baidu Apollo Rolls in the AV Industry," *EE Times*, August 4, 2022, https://www.eetimes.com/how-baidu-apollorolls-in-the-av-industry/.
48 Sarah Dai, "Baidu to build self-driving test facility in Chongqing as the Chinese city pushes ahead with smart city infrastructure," *South*

China Morning Post, March 20, 2020, https://www.scmp.com/tech/big-tech/article/3076088/baidu-build-self-driving-test-facility-chongqing-western-city-pushes.

49 "Number of self-driving testing cars in Beijing, China 2020, by company," *Statista*, March 8, 2022, https://www.statista.com/statistics/1116693/china-number-of-vehicles-for-autonomous-driving-testing-by-entity/.

50 Jane Lanhee Lee and Munsif Vengattil, "Baidu gets California nod for testing empty self-driving cars," *Reuters*, January 27, 2021, https://www.reuters.com/article/us-baidu-autonomous/baidu-gets-california-nod-for-testing-empty-self-driving-cars-idUSKBN29W2OT.

51 David Silver, "Baidu launches self-driving cars, shuttles, buses, vending and even police robots," *Forbes*, February 12, 2021, https://www.forbes.com/sites/davidsilver/2021/02/12/baidu-launches-self-driving-cars-shuttles-buses-vending-and-even-police-robots/?sh=2def5aed28c7.

52 "Android of the auto industry? How Baidu may race ahead of Google, Tesla, and others in autonomous vehicles," *CB Insights*, June 11, 2011, https://www.cbinsights.com/research/baidu-china-autonomous-vehicles/.

53 David Silver, "Baidu launches self-driving cars, shuttles, buses, vending and even police robots," *Forbes*, February 12, 2021, https://www.forbes.com/sites/davidsilver/2021/02/12/baidu-launches-self-driving-cars-shuttles-buses-vending-and-even-police-robots/?sh=2def5aed28c7.

54 There are 5 levels of driving autonomous car: level 0 with no driving automation; level 1 with driver assistance, level 2 partial automation; level 3 condition automation; level 4 high automation; level 5 full automation. Please see 6 levels of vehicle autonomy explained, Synopsis, https://www.synopsys.com/automotive/autonomous-driving-levels.html.

55 "Baidu, Guangzhou ink transport deal," Guangzhou Foreign Affairs Office, August 31, 2020, http://www.eguangzhou.gov.cn/2020-08/31/c_532507.htm.

56 Ibid.

57 "Baidu's Apollo aims to offer robotaxi service to 3 mln users in 2023," *Reuters*, June 16, 2021, https://www.reuters.com/business/autos-transportation/baidus-apollo-aims-offer-robotaxi-service-3-mln-users-2023-2021-06-17/.

58 Rita Liao, "China's search giant Baidu to set up an EV-making venture," *TechCrunch*, January 11, 2021, https://techcrunch.com/2021/01/10/baidu-electric-car-making/.

59 Arjun Kharpal, "Chinese search giant Baidu to create an electric vehicle company," *CNBC*, January 10, 2021, https://www.cnbc.com/2021/01/11/chinese-search-giant-baidu-to-create-an-electric-vehicle-company.html.

60 Evelyn Cheng, "China's booming electric car industry is much bigger than just Nio and Xpeng," *CNBC*, September 13, 2021, https://www.cnbc.com/2021/09/13/chinas-electric-car-industry-is-much-bigger-than-nio-xpeng-li-auto.html.

61 Jacky Wong, "Chinese EVs want to shock global markets next," *Wall Street Journal*, December 20, 2021, https://www.wsj.com/articles/chinese-evs-want-to-shock-global-markets-next-11639998183.

62 "EXCLUSIVE China in talks with automakers on EV subsidy extension -sources," *Reuters*, May 18, 2022, https://www.reuters.com/business/autos-transportation/exclusive-china-talks-with-automakers-ev-subsidy-extension-sources-2022-05-18/.
63 Wong, "Chinese EVs."
64 Pete Pattisson and Febriana Firdaus, "'Battery arms race': How China has monopolised the electric vehicle industry," *Guardian*, November 25, 2021, https://www.theguardian.com/global-development/2021/nov/25/battery-arms-race-how-china-has-monopolised-the-electric-vehicle-industry.
65 "Public electric vehicle charging pole number in China 2010–2021," *Statista*, April 7, 2022, https://www.statista.com/statistics/993121/china-public-electric-vehicle-charging-station-number/.
66 "Electric vehicle charging stations and outlets in U.S," *Statista*, January 13, 2022, https://www.statista.com/statistics/416750/number-of-electric-vehicle-charging-stations-outlets-united-states/.
67 Thomas Alsop, "Market revenue of artificial intelligence chips from 2020 to 2026," *Statista*, January 11, https://www.statista.com/statistics/1283358/artificial-intelligence-chip-market-size/.
68 Joy Dantong Ma, "Chip on the shoulder: How China aims to compete in semiconductors," *Marco Polo,* September 10, 2019, https://macropolo.org/china-chips-semiconductors-artificial-intelligence/?rp=e.
69 Asa Fitch and Dan Stumpft, "Blacklisting of China's top chipmaker SMIC comes with exceptions," *Wall Street Journal*, December 22, 2021, https://www.wsj.com/articles/blacklisting-of-chinas-top-chip-maker-smic-comes-with-exceptions-11608656929.
70 "Huawei, SMIC suppliers received billions worth of licenses for U.S. goods," *Reuters*, October 21, 2021, https://www.reuters.com/article/usa-china-huawei-tech-idCNL1N2RH2AC.
71 "Rise Of China's big tech in AI: What Baidu, Alibaba, and Tencent are working on," *CB Insights*, April 26, 2018, https://www.cbinsights.com/research/china-baidu-alibaba-tencent-artificial-intelligence-dominance/.
72 Nicole Kobie, "NVIDIA and the battle for the future of AI chips," *Wired*, June 17, 2021, https://www.wired.co.uk/article/nvidia-ai-chips.
73 Shen Lu, "Chinese chip companies raised a record $11 billion in 2021," *Protocol*, February 23, 2022, https://www.protocol.com/bulletins/china-chip-funding-11-billion.
74 Kate O'Keefle, Heather Somerville, and Yang Jie, "US companies aid China's bid for chip dominance despite security concerns," *Wall Street Journal*, November 12, 2021, https://www.wsj.com/articles/u-s-firms-aid-chinas-bid-for-chip-dominance-despite-security-concerns-11636718400.
75 Sun Hena, "Baidu and Samsung team up for mass production of AI chip," *Nikkei Asia*, December 20, 2019, https://asia.nikkei.com/Business/China-tech/Baidu-and-Samsung-team-up-for-mass-production-of-AI-chip.
76 David Harvey, *Marx, Capital and the Madness of Economic Reason* (New York: Oxford University Press, 2018), 124.

77 James Vincent, "Baidu launches medical chatbot to help Chinese doctors diagnose patients," *Verge*, October 11, 2016, https://www.theverge.com/2016/10/11/13240434/baidu-medical-chatbot-china-melody.
78 Sarah O'Meara, "China's data-driven dream to overhaul health care," *Nature*, October 6, 2021, https://doi-org.stanford.idm.oclc.org/10.1038/d41586-021-02694-1.
79 Arjun Kharpal, "China's Baidu is in talks to raise up to $2 billion to launch a stand-alone biotech company," *cbnc*, September 20, 2020, https://www.cnbc.com/2020/09/10/baidu-raising-money-for-biotech-firm-that-uses-artificial-intelligence-.html.
80 Ibid.
81 Xin-fa Zhou and Lu Chen, "Digital health care in China and access for older people," *The LANCET Public Health*, June 28, 2021, https://www.thelancet.com/journals/lanpub/article/PIIS2468-2667(21)00051-7/fulltext.
82 Ibid.
83 Ibid.
84 Liza Lin, "With $1.9 Billion Investment, Former Baidu Unit Challenges Fintech Rivals," *Wall Street Journal,* April 28, 2018, https://www.wsj.com/articles/with-1-9-billion-investment-former-baidu-unit-challenges-fintech-rivals-1524986810.
85 Viviana Zhu, "China's FinTech: The end of the Wild West," Institute Montaigne, April, 2021, https://www.institutmontaigne.org/en/publications/chinas-fintech-end-wild-west.
86 "China's Central Bank Governor vows more Fintech crackdown," *Bloomberg News*, October 7, 2021, https://www.bloomberg.com/news/articles/2021-10-07/china-s-central-bank-governor-vows-to-continue-fintech-crackdown.
87 "PBC sets out Fintech Development Plan for 2022 to 2025," *Moody's Analytics*, January 2, 2022, https://www.moodysanalytics.com/regulatory-news/jan-04-22-pbc-sets-out-fintech-development-plan-for-2022-to-2025.
88 Qian Zhou, "A close reading of China's Fintech Development Plan for 2022–2025," *China Briefing*, January 20, 2022, https://www.china-briefing.com/news/a-close-reading-china-fintech-development-plan-for-2022-2025/#:~:text=China%20is%20now%20the%20world's,percent%20of%20the%20global%20total.
89 "Baidu joins blockchain Bandwagon with its Project Xuperchain," *Block Chain Magazine,* January 18, 2020, https://blockchainmagazine.net/baidu-joins-blockchain-bandwagon-with-its-project-xuperchain/.

3 Political Profile

The recent People's Republic of China (PRC) "crackdown" over its tech sector was widely seen as the reassertion of China's authoritarian control over its private sector. However, through the case of Baidu's relationship with the state, this chapter reveals that the relationship between the Chinese Communist Party (CCP) and China's Internet companies is not monolithic or purely hierarchical but rather multifaceted and more dynamic than perceived in the western press. As mentioned in the introduction, the CCP is in the midst of accelerating a new major industrial policy; and its implementation of an innovation-driven economic development utilizes the enlarged private sector, and in particular, the Internet sector. Unlike its previous development phase when the PRC at first invested in large state-owned enterprises,[1] this time around the PRC is deploying private tech sectors which already have technical, capital, and infrastructure capabilities. Baidu's Internet business, AI growth sector, and its related technologies need to be situated within this light.

This chapter analyzes the intersection between Baidu's business interests and China's changing political economy. The first section of the chapter illustrates Baidu's ownership structure to demonstrate the power structure within the company and the relationship with transnational capital. The second discusses the relationship between Baidu and the CCP by examining Baidu's political circles within the government, industrial, and academic complex. Finally, the chapter shows how Baidu has attempted to expand its growth sectors by using its technical capability to collaborate with provincial governments that have been spurred by the PRC's push for "new" infrastructure hand in hand with new rules and regulations as drivers of growth.

DOI: 10.4324/9781003189893-4

Who Owns Baidu?

In August 2021, Baidu's stock price fell nearly 20% following the PRC's new regulatory impositions over Chinese tech companies.[2] This was in response to China's State Administration for Market Regulations' (SAMR) fine of $2.8 billion on Alibaba for violation of the anti-monopoly law which signaled PRC's willingness to rein in China's tech industry. [3] While the spotlight was more on Alibaba and Tencent because of their market size, Baidu was far from immune from the political winds. Baidu, along with DiDi and 10 other firms, was also hit with fines. China's tightening oversight over its domestic tech companies shook Wall Street. According to Goldman Sachs, US investors were holding roughly $1 trillion of Chinese Internet and tech stocks.[4] And the majority of Baidu's shareholders were global financial institutions and many of them are from the US. Global investors were weighing whether Baidu's stocks were worth holding on to given China's new regulations on tech companies.

Over 50% of Baidu is owned by approximately 700 institutional shareholders–including Blackrock, Inc., PRIMECAP Management, and Vanguard Group, Inc. CEO Robin Li has amassed a net wealth of $16.2 billion, and is Baidu's largest shareholder by far, with a 20% stake. The top 25 shareholders combined own around 50% of Baidu's stock, which means that no single shareholder has majority power to control the company.[5] Also, a 27% stake in Baidu is owned by the public. This is a significant size but it's not enough power to exercise company policy without collaborating with other shareholders.[6] Baidu's headquarters are in Beijing and bounded by China's jurisdiction, but the composition of shareholders illustrates that Baidu and global capital are deeply intertwined.

Baidu is not an exception; rather, the considerable Chinese Internet industry has grown entangled with transnational capital. Thus, any "decoupling" between the US and China would mean that Baidu would lose access to global capital while global investors would lose access to the most lucrative growth market in the world. Neither Baidu nor Wall Street investors want to see any collateral damage, but the inter-state rivalry complicates the interests of different units of capital. Despite PRC's new regulatory measures and current geopolitical tensions, there have been no significant signs of slowing down foreign venture-capital investment in China. As the *Wall Street Journal* reported, China remains a popular investment destination even at the height of the US government's efforts to restrict US capital flow to China.[7] In 2021, venture-capital investors poured $129 billion into more than 5,300 Chinese start-ups, and this was higher than the $115 billion in 2018.[8] Reflecting the PRC's industrial policy, what has changed is that the foreign investment toward the consumer-facing Internet sector, which had accounted for 50% of investment, has been declining while the investment on "hard tech" areas such as chips, AI, and high-end manufacturing has increased.[9] Baidu's business is also responding to the changing domestic political economy.

As Chapter 2 illustrated, Baidu has transformed itself into an AI company and has been cultivating new markets by increasingly relying on China's strategic development policy drawn heavily from the private Internet sector. Thus, as much as its global competitor Google is involved in the political realm in the US,[10] Baidu's CEO Robin Li has not been outside politics in China; rather Li and other tech entrepreneurs in China have long been active within political circles.

Government Academic-Industrial Complex

One of the major political venues where China's tech CEOs and the CCP discuss long-term political, economic and cultural agendas together is at the Chinese People's Political Consultative Conference (CPPCC), the central political advisory body of the PRC.[11] CPPCC's annual meeting is held at the same time as the plenary sessions of the National People's Congress (NPC). The CPPCC National Committee and NPC plenary sessions are collectively called the "Two Sessions." Members of the CPPCC consist of representatives from the CCP and non-CCP political parties, representatives of people's organizations, ethnic minorities, and different social groups.[12] The CPPCC offers an arena for political and business networking for private companies. The CPPCC members are not elected to their positions but are named to serve as advisers to the government and judicial organs. Members submit proposals on matters of political, economic, and social issues to draw the government's attention to issues of their interests.[13] While there is no guarantee that their proposals will be implemented; the development of the Internet giants in China shows a dynamic link to the PRC's economic and industrial policy.

Since 2013, Baidu's CEO Robin Li has been a member of CPPCC. And should be no surprise that his CPPCC proposals have consistently been about Baidu's own business interests promulgating

AI technologies, autonomous vehicles (AVs) and associated issues. During the 2015 CPPCC meeting, Li proposed the establishment of a state-level AI project called "China brain." He urged the CPPCC to bring together the scientific community, military, and private companies and stated "I hope China can mobilize the resources of the whole nation to develop the biggest AI development platform in the world."[14] Li expressed that the project should be at the same level as US research projects like the Manhattan Project, the Apollo program, and the Human Genome Project.[15] He requested that the government support companies which are able to build open platforms offering AI-related basic resources and public services[16] and suggested that the CPPCC could pursue this through market mechanisms to transform AI research into commercial products and integrate AI technologies into traditional industries, the service sector, and the military.[17]

Coincidently or not, less than two years after Li's proposal, the National Development and Reform Commission of China (NDRC) approved the creation of the National Engineering Laboratory for Deep Learning Technology and Applications. The laboratory was established on Baidu's campus in Shangdi, a district designated by the Beijing municipal government as the center of the city's information technology industry.[18] The lab is led by the company and focuses on large-scale industrialized AI products and artificial intelligence application technology in collaboration with major elite universities including Tsinghua University, Beijing University of Aeronautics and Astronautics, the China Academy of Information and Communications Technology, and China Electronics Technology Standardization Institute.[19] Baidu's partnership with the Institute for AI Industry Research (AIR) at Tsinghua University introduced *Apollo Air*, a platform for *Vehicle to Everything* (V2X) that was tested in Beijing, Guangzhou, and Cangzhou. As of this writing, Haifeng Wang, Baidu's current CTO and former chief research scientist at Toshiba's R&D Center, is the president of the lab.[20] The reason for the NDRC's quick approval was because Baidu had already been long invested in R&D in the field of AI.

In 2013, Baidu established the Institute of Deep Learning (IDL) within the Baidu Research division, the first AI research institute in China and had also created branches in Beijing, Shanghai, Shenzhen, Seattle, and Silicon Valley. In 2014, Baidu announced that it would invest $300 million to start a new R&D center in Silicon Valley with 200 employees.[21] In particular, Baidu set up a research lab in Silicon Valley for strategic reasons because the

Valley is the hub where Baidu could access a pool of scientists and engineers, new technologies and access to capital.[22] As the company built its 1,300-person AI research team over the years, Baidu recruited Andrew Ng who was an associate professor at Stanford University and Director of the Stanford AI Lab.[23] Ng had founded Google's deep learning research project *Google Brain* and is considered one of the top AI scientists in the world. Ng as chief scientist led Baidu's AI research group until 2017. He left five years ago, but opened a talent pipeline to draw in needed AI engineers from the Valley for Baidu.[24] With his departure, Baidu hired Qi Lu as the chief operating officer who was a former executive at Microsoft and an AI specialist. Subsequently, in 2018 Baidu Research created an advisory board heavily drawing from US academia and industry.[25]

Over several years, Baidu, like its major US tech counterparts, has been building out and expanding its partnerships with state, domestic, and US universities, and domestic and international companies to strengthen the company's strategic growth sectors. Baidu is an inner-circle resident within the academic, government, and industrial complex in China and beyond. Similar to how the US tech companies like Google, Amazon, Apple, and Facebook influence the shaping of the US political economic agenda, the close relationship between the scions of the Chinese tech industry and PRC's economic policy are evident and obviously noticeable with the heavy presence of tech companies at the CPPCC.

Along with incumbents Baidu, Alibaba, and Tencent, the PRC invited a slew of new tech CEOs and entrepreneurs as new CPPCC members at the 2018 CPPCC meeting. The newcomers joining the meeting were mobile game publisher *NetEase*, e-commerce operator *JD.com*, cybersecurity business and search company *Qihoo 360*, the second largest search engine *Sogou*, and Chinese mobile manufacturer *Xiaomi*'s CEO Lei Jun.[26] It was indicative that the PRC was assembling private tech companies to be involved in the process of creating China's new national economic objectives. In that meeting, many of the tech companies submitted their own proposals of interest. Baidu's CEO Li put forward a proposal for a national development fund for the self-driving car industry and urged the CPPCC to have a national policy to industrialize the industry, improve data security for autonomous driving, develop a national AI platform, and create a preferential tax policy.[27] Lenovo's CEO pitched the development of Beijing AI city deploying AI as an economic growth engine.[28] Meanwhile, Tencent's Pony Ma urged the group to digitize traditional industrial sectors implementing cloud,

Internet infrastructures, etc.[29] For Baidu, in order to commercialize its growth sector of AVs and EVs on a mass scale, the company needs digital infrastructure – 5G, road maintenance, advanced traffic information and management, and storage and charging facilities.[30] Li has recommended that the government speed up the construction of a national AI infrastructure and smart transportation and apply the open-source deep learning platform across the industry.[31] Using this official venue, tech companies have signaled for government support of necessary infrastructure and laws and regulations that are friendly to their business environments.[32]

These proposals by the Internet giants are not far departed from the CCPs' new industrial policy that emphasizes the application of next-generation technologies to upgrade its industrial base. However, this diverts from a widely held view that China's private sectors are under threat by the PRC's recent wide-ranging regulatory imposition. Indeed, new policies are being instituted to rein in tech heavyweights' monopolistic expansion, but there is no evidence yet that China's private tech companies are retreating from the market.[33] Barry Naughton describes China's new economic development as "grand steerage" in which the government and state authorities steer China's national economy to a high-tech economy encompassing new infrastructure that is embedded with sensors, smart grids, 5G, AI, "urbanization 2.0," supply chain initiatives and semiconductor investment.[34] This view is not entirely incorrect because the PRC is indeed trying to redirect the course of the economic development; however, this view highlights the PRC's top-down only approach. In reality, the process involves both cooperation and discord with counter-pressures from local governments, domestic private tech companies, transnational capital, and different political fractions.

Thus, rather than just have the central government lead in the implementation of a national industrial strategy, decentralized local provincial governments supported by the CCP, have been enticing domestic private Internet companies and foreign investors with a series of subsidies including R&D funding, tax incentives, building infrastructure and favorable regulatory environments in strategic areas such as AI, AVs, EVs, cloud computing, and chip production to encourage new technology development and applications.[35] Besides subsidies, local governments compete among each other and forges strategic relationships with Internet companies – which is a more valuable proposition for companies as the partnerships provide access to long-term markets and favorable government treatment.[36] Baidu has been in pursuit of partnerships with local governments as the PRC is accelerating digital industrialization by deeper integration of digital technology into traditional industries.

New Infrastructure

To support digital industrialization, the PRC is restructuring and upgrading China's industrial base, massively rolling out network infrastructures in Chinese provinces to enable applications and services over the infrastructure under the concept of "new infrastructure" to distinguish from traditional roads and bridges.[37] New infrastructure encompasses three key areas: new information infrastructure which includes 5G, IoT, the industrial Internet, satellite Internet, AI, cloud, data centers; "integrated/fused infrastructure" which means the application of the Internet, and big data to upgrade traditional infrastructure like transportation and "smart" energy facilities; and "innovation infrastructure" which refers to public infrastructure that supports education and R&D.[38]

Baidu is one of the leading companies benefiting from the state's infrastructure push as its AI and cloud businesses cut cross this massive new initiative. Considering that Baidu's international market is limited, the company's biggest market is naturally domestic, in particular, the central government and, by extension, local governments whose development projects are heavily centered around bolstering the development and application of advanced technologies across economic sectors. Baidu's core business of AI-enabled automobiles sits at the center of China's strategic industries for new infrastructure development. In fact, the AV industry is fueled, facilitated, and encouraged by part of the CCP's "new infrastructure" projects as it involves 5G, application of AI, big data, industrial Internet and upgrading of traditional sectors. In the 14th Five Year Plan (FYP), the digitization of autonomous driving and smart transport was identified as a key area of development.[39] The Plan called to "develop travel services for autonomous driving and vehicle-road collaboration travel services. Promote intelligent highway , traffic signal linkage, and bus priority control... [and] build [...] smart parking lots."[40]

Baidu was already named as one of China's AI national champions along with Alibaba and Tencent. These three were designated as a "national team" by China's Ministry of Science and Technology (MOST).[41] Specifically, Baidu has been assigned to develop and commercialize autonomous driving, Alibaba has been charged with cloud for smart cities, while Tencent is to focus on medical imaging and iFlyTek for voice recognition.[42] The Chinese government encourages private companies to invest in their products and develop technologies; meanwhile the state facilitates the building of public network infrastructure and services where tech companies can deploy their technologies and commercialize them. Along with domestic companies, Chinese policies on AC also calls for foreign investment in several areas such as R&D and manufacturing of AV components, and hardware. [43] Unlike during the 2008 global economic crisis when the PRC led the massive investment in traditional infrastructure, this time around, the state is relying on market forces and drawing heavily from the private tech sectors in restructuring its economy through advancing and building digital "new" infrastructure. China's public and private sectors together are planning to spend $1.6 trillion through 2025 to develop their next-generation infrastructure.[44]

Baidu is making inroads in collaborating with local governments on investment of AI infrastructure. In Wuhu city, where the local government relaxed its regulations so that the company could experiment with AVs, Baidu signed an agreement in 2016 to jointly build a pilot driverless car testing zone.[45] In 2019, Baidu's self-driving arm *Apollo* along with two other companies received a license for commercial operations from the city of Wuhan to operate the first 5G-based driverless commercial bus service.[46] The local government partnered with China Mobile and telecom equipment giant Huawei Technologies to build the necessary wireless infrastructure combining 5G and the Beidou Chinese satellite navigation system.[47] Baidu is working with China Mobile to access the "5G + BeiDou" for its map service which supports lane navigation for AVs. The PRC has been pushing the development and use of Beidou to compete in the highly lucrative and crucial satellite navigation market against the US government-owned Global Positioning System (GPS) which has historically dominated the standard satellite navigation system.[48] Beidou and 5G networks are key strategic technologies that are integrated into AV infrastructure.

Baidu forged a series of strategic alliances with major cities which are competing to launch robotaxi programs as part of their new infrastructure plans. Cities which introduced the programs included Beijing, Changsha in Hunan province, and Cangzhou in Hebei province.[49] In 2020, Baidu signed agreements to build a major smart transportation project in Guangzhou, the capital of Guangdong province. Baidu's subsidiary, Guangzhou Apollo Intelligent Transportation Co. Ltd., is cooperating with the Guangzhou-based Sci Group and Guangzhou Public Transport Group to develop joint self-driving and smart transport projects encompassing robotaxis and 5G-powered robobuses for public transportation.[50] The Baidu service has already launched in 2020 in the metropolis of Chongqing where Baidu built its testing facility in collaboration with the Chongqing municipal government that includes sensors, traffic signal control systems, edge computing, and data storage capabilities.[51] In 2022, Baidu launched its operation of driverless taxis in Chongqing and Wuhan, becoming the first company to run fully autonomous taxis without any human drivers on board.[52]

One of China's most prominent infrastructure projects in which Baidu is actively participating is the construction of a brand new city from scratch named Xiong'an New Area (Xiong'an) in Hebei province located to the south of Beijing. Xiong'an is listed as part of one of the regional strategies in the 14th FYP. In 2017, the PRC announced the project which aimed to integrate the Beijing Tianjin-Hebei city-region creating a special zone to alleviate intra-region inequality and the problems to surrounding areas of large urban cities such as pollution, transportation, population, and housing. Different from other special zones, Xiong'an will only invite technology firms, ban the building of factories, and won't allow large scale real estate sales. The project is designed to transform Xiong'an area from an agriculture and low-end manufacturing area to a digital metropolis and technology hub where IoT technologies, AI, big data, blockchain, and cloud computing have been encouraged in the planning and design of the city. All housing in the area will be owned by the state and will be provided at a subsidized rate to people who work in Xiong'an.[53] It is estimated to cost $580 billion in infrastructure over the next 20 years.

To pursue the Xiong'an mega project, the PRC brought all the major private tech companies to the new city. In 2017, Baidu signed an agreement with Xiong'an Administrative Committee to set up a national AI laboratory and transform its economic zone into an AI city, integrating AVs, smart traffic lights, and parking.[54] Baidu, Alibaba, and Tencent all established their outposts in Xiong'an where the local government has created conditions for competition and collaboration to develop the city. Major Chinese telecommunication companies China Mobile, Unicom, and China Telecom are working together to test their 5G network in the area.[55] The PRC has deployed urban development as an integral national economic strategy to incorporate new technologies and upgrade its industrial sectors, drawing on China's major private tech companies. Baidu is eager to take a piece of the State's tech-driven urban development project and has been testing its own 5G-connected self-driving cars in the region.

With the expansion of new digital infrastructure building across economic, social sectors and cities, new regulations that are associated with new infrastructure – including data protection, storage, and security laws – have become necessary to accommodate the new emerging sectors. Baidu has urged the CCP to provide this new regulatory framework conducive to supporting AI-driven digital infrastructure.

New Regulations Paving the Way

At the 2016 CCPPC meeting, CEO Li proposed that regulations, industry standards and policies needed to be updated in order to support and develop next-generation technologies like AI and AVs. Pointing out the necessity of regulations to develop AVs, he wrote, "more Chinese companies are investing in driverless car R&D, but related regulations and policies lag behind."[56] The chairman of Chinese automaker Zhejiang Geely Holding Group, Baidu's EV partner, submitted a similar proposal to the CCP, urging the party to set up a legal framework for self-driving cars.[57] In fact, in 2017, Li was fined for driving AVs on a Beijing Highway, because AVs were illegal on public roads at the time.[58] In Baidu's 2019 annual report, the company wrote several times and addressed their concerns about regulatory uncertainty in the operation of their AI-related businesses.[59] The lack of rules and regulations are not only barriers to domestic companies like Baidu but also foreign companies who are eager to enter into the largest automobile market in the world. China's recent slew of data regulations over tech companies should be seen within this context.

Before the central government pushed out its official regulations, local governments, endorsed by the central government, were competing to draft their own local rules and regulations to speed up the development of AVs and allow them to operate on public roads. In December 2017, Beijing became the first Chinese city to allow AV road testing. In the following year, China's Ministry of Transportation gave the approving nod for all provincial and city governments to test AVs on their public roads. In 2018, China's National Development and Reform Commission and the Ministry of Industry and Information Technology (MIIT), along with several other government agencies, released a draft strategic plan to complete its standards for AVs and infrastructure, legislation, supervision, and network safety by 2025.[60]

To accelerate the development of the AV industry, the PRC released new regulations on data regarding the handling of self-driving cars. In 2021, the PRC issued its Regulation on Security Management of Automotive Data which tightened the collection and management of different types of data – personal data generated in China and other "critical/important data" throughout the operation of the industry including AV design, city mapping, automobile and pedestrian traffic, and audiovisual data from cameras and sensors for AVs etc.[61] This industry specific regulation was part of the umbrella of China's three key data regulations: 2017 Cyber Security Law, new Data Security Law (DSL), and the Personal Information Protection Law (PIPL), the latter two had come into effect at the end of 2021.[62] The new auto data regulation will be a significant hurdle to collect personal and "critical" data involved in the process of AV design, production, operation, and maintenance.[63]

Considering Baidu is involved in an array of Internet businesses that collect personal data, the company is not just affected by DSL but also has to comply with PIPL modeled on the EU's General Data Protection Regulation (GDPR) law.[64] PIPL lays out how data can be collected, used, and stored, as well as setting up data processing requirements for companies operating outside of China. In the case of a PIPL violation, the company would be fined $7.8 million, or 5% of the company's annual revenue.[65] PIPL is considered to be stricter data regulation than the GDPR law passed in 2018.

Baidu hasn't commented publicly about the new data regulations. However, there is little question that these new regulations will negatively affect Baidu and other Internet companies' bottom lines of their core businesses. After all, mass data collection is central for their capital accumulation of both their current Internet businesses as well as new AI sectors including AVs. Wang Haifeng, Vice President of Baidu, reaffirmed the point stating, "data is the lifeblood of AI, and in China, we have excellent data pools."[66] In 2018, CEO Li was under fire for stating at the China Development Forum in Beijing, "I think that the Chinese people are more open, or not so sensitive, about the privacy issue. If they are able to exchange privacy for convenience or efficiency, they are willing to do so in many cases."[67] This was a reflection on how Baidu has long treated personal data for their business. In the same year, the Jiangsu Consumer Council filed a lawsuit against Baidu for illegally collecting data without consent – the Council later withdrew the suit after Baidu removed the function of its apps that collects user data.[68] Moreover, Beijing had already nudged the company to stop its illegal data collection. Throughout 2021, the Cyberspace Administration of China (CAC) called out tech companies for illegally collecting user data on mobile apps, and warned them to correct it and comply with the new regulations.[69] The MIIT removed more than 100 apps from Chinese app stores for privacy violations, and subsequently listed 106 apps that violated the data collection regulations.[70] The CAC also put on notice for violating data privacy regulations 33 Mapping and text apps including Baidu Map, Alibaba's AutoNavi, Tencent, and China's home-grown satellite navigation system BeiDou.[71]

The CCP's sweeping data regulations seem contradictory to the state's claim of the importance of the tech sector; the new regulations negatively affect the Internet companies that generate profit by exploiting personal data and the cost of doing business in China. Indeed, the data regulations allow the CCP to further exercise power over the tech companies while remaining at arm's length. However, China's regulatory reforms do not mean that the PRC is seizing control of the private tech sector. The Western media has often portrayed the new data regulations as CCP's increasing power over the private sector, censorship, and the reining in of China's oversized tech industry. This perspective is not completely false; however, this doesn't offer a full picture. The data governance rules function more than on the protection of individual privacy and illegal data collection practices. The regulations are also tightly connected to economic and trade issues, including a clause on controlling the movement of data outside the Chinese territory. This applies to both domestic companies and China's foreign competitors. In response to regulatory changes, companies like Tesla have already complied with the new regulations to store their data locally and have increased the capacity of their local data centers in China.[72] Data regulations are also deployed to create market certainty to draw foreign capital, barriers for trade to protect domestic markets, and give domestic companies a competitive edge by formulating policy standards, creating trade barriers, and controlling foreign access to China's digital market.[73]

China's data regulatory actions are a broader part of China's new phase of economic development aiming to boost its global competitiveness. To that end, along with the US and Europe, China has joined a growing number of countries that are regulating technology sectors from data protection to antitrust. In particular, the EU has been weaponizing regulations to challenge the dominance of the US tech companies in Europe while trying to create space for European-based tech companies. Thus, despite a short-term negative impact on China's domestic Internet industry built on data, the underlying logic behind China's regulatory move is to lay out the foundation for its new phase of economic development in which next-generation technologies are the principle driving forces and will be integrated into all areas of production. Over the decades, Baidu and its rivals enjoyed little oversight, and this facilitated their rapid expansion. The CCP sees that new regulations on data are a necessary step in order to usher in a new phase of long-term domestic economic development focused on the industrial Internet, one that will continue to be accepting of foreign capital and with a goal of gaining a strategic position within the global capitalist system. Baidu's Internet business is both constrained as well as dynamically expanded within China's changing political economy.

Conclusion

This chapter shows that Baidu's ownership and its finances are deeply rooted in complex global capital and financial institutions, but Baidu's business is also tightly interlinked to the domestic political economy. In particular, to further its AI business, Baidu has employed its long-cultivated network within the government, academic, and industrial complex. At CPPCC, where Baidu's CEO Robin Li and his tech rivals and alliances are notably present, companies have lobbied for their own corporate agendas; therefore, Li has been pressing Baidu's own business interests and urging the state to integrate AI technologies across economic sectors and accelerate a national level AVs industry development, supporting necessary infrastructure, favorable markets, and regulatory conditions. Meanwhile, the CCP is trying to mobilize technically capable private Internet companies as it reorients its economic development strategies focusing on capital-intensive "new" infrastructure. This has also been the reason for the party state's setting of a series of new regulations which have accordingly affected the bottom lines of the Internet companies' existing consumer-oriented businesses. The new wave of regulations has constrained the relationship between the CCP and the private sector. This could be seen as the CCP's reassertion of control over the sector and the private enterprises with a move back to SOEs; however, the private sector is far from declining in power or influence.

Despite the setback from the new regulatory regimes, Baidu has also been benefiting from the CCP's new industrial policy as the state has been incentivizing the private companies to invest in new strategic sectors such as AI, semiconductors, block chain, data centers, batteries, etc. Baidu is promulgating its AI businesses through close alliances with local digital infrastructure initiatives backed by the central government. Considering Baidu's core search business has been stagnant, and its revenue is still largely coming from within China, the domestic market is vital for Baidu's future growth. However, this doesn't imply that Baidu is a proxy of the CCP; rather, as Lianrui Jia and Dwayne Winseck state, the Internet companies like Baidu should be seen as capitalist enterprises which operate under an expansionist imperative and are tightly woven into the global capital market.[74] Baidu is trying to position itself to ensure growth and shore up its market share within the changing domestic political economic and geopolitical context as the party state is maneuvering among inter-capitalist state competition, domestic social and economic dynamics, national interests, and the interests of domestic and global capital.

Notes

1 Dieter Ernst and Barry Naughton, "China's Emergent Political Economy – Insights from the IT Industry," in *China's Emergent Political Economy – Capitalism in the Dragon's Lair*, ed. Christopher A. McNally (London: Routledge, 2008), 39.
2 James Brumley, "Why Baidu fell nearly 20% in July," *Nasdaq*, August 4, 2021, https://www.nasdaq.com/articles/why-baidu-fell-nearly-20-in-july-2021-08-04.
3 Raymond Zhong, "China Fines Alibaba $2.8 Billion in Landmark Antitrust Case," *New York Times*, April 9, 2021, https://www.nytimes.com/2021/04/09/technology/china-alibaba-monopoly-fine.html.
4 Marc Jones, "Analysis: The trillion dollar weapon in the U.S.-China tech stock war," *Reuters*, January 12, 2021, https://www.reuters.com/article/us-china-usa-listings-indexes-analysis/analysis-the-trillion-dollar-weapon-in-the-u-s-china-tech-stock-war-idUSKBN29H20P.
5 "What is the ownership structure like for Baidu, Inc.?" *Nasdaq*, May 14, 2021, https://www.nasdaq.com/articles/what-is-the-ownershipstructure-like-for-baidu-inc.-nasdaq%3Abidu-2021-05-14.
6 Ibid.

7 Liza Lin, Jing Yang, and Keith Zhai, "China's startups are awash with money as Beijing shifts focus to 'Hard Tech'," *Wall Street Journal*, January 13, 2020, https://www.wsj.com/articles/chinas-startups-attract-record-funding-despite-tech-clampdown-11642000017.
8 Ibid.
9 Ibid.
10 Alphabet Inc., Open Secret, 2021, https://www.opensecrets.org/federal-lobbying/clients/summary?id=D000067823.
11 "Roles and functions of Chinese people's political consultative conference," The National Committee of The Chinese People's Political Consultative Conference, August 26, 2021, http://en.cppcc.gov.cn/2020-03/17/c_470023.htm.
12 Ibid.
13 Ibid.
14 Zang Rui, "Baidu CEO proposes National AI Project," *China Today*, March 15, 2015, http://www.china.org.cn/china/NPC_CPPCC_2015/2015-03/12/content_35030729.htm.
15 Ibid.
16 Elsa Kania, "China's AI agenda advances," *The Diplomate*, February 14, 2018, https://thediplomat.com/2018/02/chinas-ai-agenda-advances/.
17 Bien Perez, "'China Brain' project seeks military funding as Baidu makes artificial intelligence plans," *South China Morning*, March 2, 2015, https://www.scmp.com/lifestyle/article/1728422/china-brain-project-seeks-military-funding-baidu-makes-artificial.
18 Meghan Han and Rita Chen, "China's National Engineering Laboratory of deep learning technology was established at Baidu Campus: We are the national team of deep learning," *Synced,* March 27, 2017, https://medium.com/syncedreview/chinas-national-engineering-laboratory-of-deep-learning-technology-was-established-at-baidu-campus-8db098fedd4e.
19 "Deep learning technology and applications," STIP Compass, November 20, 2019, https://stip.oecd.org/stip/interactive-dashboards/policy-initiatives/2021%2Fdata%2FpolicyInitiatives%2F16868.
20 "Baidu research establishes an advisory board, holds 1st board meeting in Silicon Valley," *Baidu Research blog*, November 15, 2018, http://research.baidu.com/Blog/index-view?id=108.
21 Paul Mozur and Rolfe Winkler, "Baidu to open Artificial-Intelligence Center in Silicon Valley," *Wall Street Journal*, May 16, 2014, https://www.wsj.com/articles/SB10001424052702304908304579565950123054242.
22 Daniela Hernandez, "'Chinese Google' opens Artificial-Intelligence Lab in Silicon Valley," *Wired, Magazine*, April 12, 2013, https://www.wired.com/2013/04/baidu-research-lab/.
23 Paul Mozur, "A.I. Expert at Baidu, Andrew Ng, resigns from Chinese search giant," *New York Times*, March 22, 2017, https://www.nytimes.com/2017/03/22/business/baidu-artificial-intelligence-andrew-ng.html.
24 Li Yuan, "China is losing to the U.S. in high-stakes battle for artificial intelligence talent," *Wall Street Journal*, March 23, 2017, https://www.wsj.com/articles/baidus-loss-is-a-setback-for-ai-in-china-149027041.
25 The initial board members were Dr. David Belanger, former Chief Scientist and Vice President at AT&T Labs; David Forsyth, Professor of

Computer Science at the University of Illinois at Urbana-Champaign; Mark Liberman, Christopher H. Browne, Professor of Linguistics at the University of Pennsylvania; Martial Hebert, Director of the Robotics Institute at Carnegie Mellon University; and Vipin Kumar, Regents Professor and William Norris Chair in Large-Scale Computing at the University of Minnesota. See "Baidu research bolsters capabilities with new labs and world-renowned appointment to advisory board," *Baidu Blog,* July 2, 2019, http://research.baidu.com/Blog/index-view?id=120.

26 "The First Session of the 13th CPPCC National Committee," The National Committee of the Chinese People's Political Consultative Conference, http://en.cppcc.gov.cn/1stsessionofthe13thcppccncproposals.html.

27 "Baidu's Li calls for investment fund to boost self-driving sector," *China Daily*, March 6, 2018, http://en.cppcc.gov.cn/2018-03/06/c_571615.htm.

28 Yimian Wu, "Tech entrepreneurs a growing force at China's communist party meeting," *China Money Network*, March 5, 2018, https://www.chinamoneynetwork.com/2018/03/05/tech-entrepreneurs-growing-force-chinas-communist-party-meeting.

29 Xie Yu and Sidney Leng, "Tech entrepreneurs replace real estate tycoons as political advisers in China's push for IT edge," *South China Morning Post*, March 4, 2018, https://www.scmp.com/business/companies/article/2135642/tech-entrepreneurs-replace-real-estate-tycoons-political-advisers.

30 Tyler Duvall, Eric Hannon, Jared Katseff, Ben Safran, and Tyler Wallace, "A new look at autonomous-vehicle infrastructure," *McKinsey & Company*, May 22, 2019, https://www.mckinsey.com/industries/travel-logistics-and-infrastructure/our-insights/a-new-look-at-autonomous-vehicle-infrastructure.

31 Song Jingli, "This is what Chinese tech tycoons brought to the table at China's two sessions," *KrAisa*, May 27, 2020, https://kr-asia.com/what-chinese-tech-tycoons-brought-to-the-table-during-chinas-two-sessions.

32 Shunsuke Tabeta, "Internet executives well represented at China's National Congress," *Asia Nikkei*, March 7, 2018, https://asia.nikkei.com/Spotlight/China-People-s-Congress-2018/Internet-executives-well-represented-at-China-s-National-Congress.

33 Tianlei Huang and Nicolas Véron, "The private sector advances in China," Peterson Institute for International Economics, March 22, https://www.piie.com/sites/default/files/documents/wp22-3.pdf.

34 Barry Naughton, "Grand Steerage," in *Fateful Decisions Choices That Will Shape China's Future*, ed. Thomas Fingar and Jean C. Oi (Stanford California: Stanford University Press, 2022), 51–81.

35 Yujia He, "How China is preparing for an AI-powered future," *Wilson Brief*, June 2017, https://www.wilsoncenter.org/sites/default/files/media/documents/publication/how_china_is_preparing_for_ai_powered_future.pdf.

36 Kathy Gao, "Where next for China's technology policy? Creating the industrial internet," *Bloomberg NEF*, December 9, 2019, https://about.bnef.com/blog/where-next-for-chinas-technology-policy-creating-the-industrial-internet/.

37 Paul Triolo and Allison Sherlock, "'New infrastructure' – China's race for 5G and networked everything has a new catchphrase," *SupChina*, July 1, 2020, https://supchina.com/2020/07/01/new-infrastructure-chinas-race-for-5g-and-networked-everything-has-a-new-catchphrase/.

38 Ibid.

39 Outline of the People's Republic of China 14th Five-Year Plan for National Economic and Social Development and Long-Range Objectives for 2035, trans, *Xinhua News Agency*, March 12, 2021, https://cset.georgetown.edu/wp-content/uploads/t0284_14th_Five_Year_Plan_EN.pdf.

40 Ibid.

41 Benjamin Larsen, "Drafting China's National AI Team for governance," *New America*, November 19, 2019, https://www.newamerica.org/cybersecurity-initiative/digichina/blog/drafting-chinas-national-ai-team-governance/.

42 Ibid.

43 Arendse Huld, "China's autonomous driving industry – An introduction for foreign investors," *China Briefing*, October 26, 2021, https://www.china-briefing.com/news/investing-in-chinas-self-driving-car-market/.

44 Takashi Kawakami, "China to pump $1.6tn into tech infrastructure through 2025," *Nikkei Asia*, January 21, 2021, https://asia.nikkei.com/Business/China-tech/China-to-pump-1.6tn-into-tech-infrastructure-through-2025.

45 "Chinese city Wuhu embraces driverless vehicles," *BBC*, May 16, 2016, https://www.bbc.com/news/technology-36301911.

46 Shusuke Tabeta, "Baidu wins China's first commercial license for self-driving buses," *Asia Nikkei*, September 26, 2019, https://asia.nikkei.com/Business/Automobiles/Baidu-wins-China-s-first-commercial-license-for-self-driving-buses.

47 Ibid.

48 Yen Nee Lee, "China races to rival the U.S. with its own GPS system – but one analyst says it won't overtake the U.S. yet," *CNBC*, March 31, 2021, https://www.cnbc.com/2021/06/01/tech-war-chinas-beidou-gains-market-share-challenges-us-gps.html.

49 Li Fusheng, "Baidu offers autonomous vehicle service in Guangzhou," *China Daily*, February 9, 2021, https://www.chinadaily.com.cn/a/202102/09/WS60222825a31024ad0baa8568.html.

50 Qiu Quanlin, "Baidu, Guangzhou ink transport deal,' *China Daily*, August 29, 2020, https://global.chinadaily.com.cn/a/202008/29/WS5f49b815a310675eafc563cf.html.

51 Sarah Dai, "Baidu to build self-driving test facility in Chongqing as the Chinese City pushes ahead with Smart City infrastructure," *South China Morning Post*, March 20, 2020, https://www.scmp.com/tech/big-tech/article/3076088/baidu-build-self-driving-test-facility-chongqing-western-city-pushes.

52 Daniel Ren, "Baidu launches China's first driverless taxi services in Chongqing and Wuhan in landmark moment for autonomous motoring," *South China Morning Post*, August 8. 2022, https://www.scmp.com/business/china-business/article/3188190/baidu-launches-chinas-first-driverless-taxi-services.

53 Cheng Li and Gary Xie, "A brave New World: Xi's Xiong'an," Brookings, April 20, 2018, https://www.brookings.edu/opinions/a-brave-new-world-xis-xiongan/.
54 Fan Feifei, "Baidu to roll out AI lab, smart transportation in Xiongan," *China Daily*, December 20, 2017, http://www.chinadaily.com.cn/a/201712/20/WS5a3a6736a31008cf16da27bd.html.
55 Frank Ka-Ho Wong, "Xiong'an New Area: President Xi's Dream City," *China Briefing*, March 26, 2019, https://www.china-briefing.com/news/xiongan-new-area-beijing-tianjin-hebei/.
56 "Internet Businessman proposes support for driverless cars," *Xinhua*, March 3, 2016, http://en.people.cn/n3/2016/0303/c90785-9024649.html.
57 Gao Yuan, "Standards sought for self-driving cars," *China Daily*, March 4, 2016, https://www.chinadaily.com.cn/china/2016twosession/2016-03/04/content_23733386.htm.
58 Benjamin Haas, "Caught no-handed: China tech CEO faces fine after driverless car stunt," *Guardian*, July 6, 2017, https://www.theguardian.com/world/2017/jul/06/caught-no-handed-china-tech-ceo-faces-fine-after-driverless-car-stunt.
59 Baidu, Annual Report, 2019, 7.
60 Mark Schaub and Atticus Zhao, "China Releases Big Plan for Autonomous Vehicles," *China Law Insight*, March 4, 2020, https://www.chinalawinsight.com/2020/03/articles/corporate-ma/china-releases-big-plan-for-autonomous-vehicles/.
61 "China's Internet of Vehicles – New Guidelines Set Framework for Industry Standards," *China Briefing*, March 15, 2022, https://www.china-briefing.com/news/china-internet-of-vehicles-new-guidelines-set-framework-for-industry-standards/.
62 China's Data Laws and Impact on the Automotive Industry, *Morgan Lewis*, March 31, 2022, https://www.morganlewis.com/pubs/2022/03/chinas-data-laws-and-impact-on-the-automotive-industry.
63 Ibid.
64 "What is GDPR, the EU's new data protection law?" GDPR.eu, https://gdpr.eu/what-is-gdpr/.
65 "10 ways China's new data rules will change your business," *PWC*, November 22, 2021, https://www.pwc.com/us/en/tech-effect/cybersecurity/china-pipl-rules-impact.html.
66 Owen Churchill, "China's AI dreams," *Nature*, January 17, 2018, https://www.nature.com/articles/d41586-018-00539-y?WT.feed_name=subjects_computer-science.
67 Liang Chenyu, "Are Chinese people 'Less Sensitive' about privacy?" *Sixth Tone*, May 27, 2018, https://www.sixthtone.com/news/1001996/are-chinese-people-less-sensitive-about-privacy%3F.
68 Winston Ma, "China awakens to digital privacy concerns," *East Asia Forum*, September 7, 2020, https://www.eastasiaforum.org/2020/09/07/china-awakens-to-digital-privacy-concerns/.
69 "China says 33 apps break rules in gathering user information," *Bloomberg*, April 30, 2021, https://www.bloomberg.com/news/articles/2021-05-01/china-says-33-apps-break-rules-in-gathering-personal-information.

70 Huan Zhu, "MIIT orders the removal of 106 apps from App Stores," *China Trade Monitor*, December 9, 2021, https://www.chinatrademonitor.com/miit-orders-to-remove-106-apps-from-app-store/.
71 Masha Borak, "China's regulator names 33 apps including Baidu, Sogou, iFlytek, Tencent for unauthorised data collection," *South China Morning*, May 1, 2021, https://www.scmp.com/tech/policy/article/3131878/chinas-regulator-names-33-apps-including-baidu-sogou-iflytek-tencent.
72 "Tesla will store Chinese car data locally, following government fears about spying," *Reuters*, May 25, 2021, https://www.reuters.com/technology/tesla-launches-china-data-centre-store-data-locally-2021-05-25/.
73 Pari Esfandiari, "Data: Governance and Geopolitics," Center for Strategies & International Studies, January 22, 2021, https://www.csis.org/analysis/data-governance-and-geopolitics.
74 Lianrui Jia and Dwayne Winseck, "The Political Economy of Chinese Internet Companies: Financialization, Concentration, and Capitalization," *International Communication Gazette*, 80, no.1 (January 2018): 30–59.

4 Cultural Profile

The function of search is as an entry point to the Internet where culture is accessed, shaped, and reshaped. Leveraging its search, network infrastructure, and technical capabilities, Baidu is expanding its business concerns into an array of traditional cultural domains – books, museums, music, TV, and films. By discussing Baidu's cultural profile, this chapter will show how the cultural sphere is being digitized and restructured into a growing economic sector and how market logics have extended into cultural domains that were once outside the market. The Chinese cultural industry has often been seen as a tool in the People's Republic of China (PRC)'s ideological weaponry; however, beyond its censorship and propaganda framework, this chapter shows how Baidu is commercializing and commodifying culture, and reorganizing cultural space to augment its profit domain.

The chapter highlights three different cultural realms where Baidu is carving out space for its profit-making. The first sphere is the "sharing culture" or "knowledge culture" in which user-generated content is being copyrighted and deployed in Baidu's search business. Adopting a western Web 2.0 business model which celebrates the notion of consumer as producer,[1] Baidu heavily relies on volunteer labor along with waged labor to extend its commercial logic into knowledge and cultural content that ultimately feeds into its ads business. The second realm shows how Baidu is commodifying culture through digitizing and marketizing cultural institutions which once were outside the market. Thirty years ago, Herbert Schiller envisaged increasing corporate power over cultural expression and public-sector cultural institutions as political economy further oriented toward information and communication.[2] This trend is not limited to the US and has accelerated across the globe. As the Chinese state has stimulated domestic information and cultural consumption as key to its economic policy, culture in China

DOI: 10.4324/9781003189893-5

has transformed into an industry that needs to be developed.[3] The third segment of Baidu's profit-making strategy involves Baidu's streaming platform *iQiyi*, a major player in China's bourgeoning streaming industry which is digitizing and restructuring China's existing entertainment industry. iQiyi demonstrates the competitive dynamics of the streaming industry in China which have driven the Chinese government to strengthen their intellectual property regime and spurred transnationalization even as iQiyi has struggled to expand in the global entertainment market.

"Sharing" Culture

Today, China's private Internet giants increasingly occupy the Chinese cultural space, leveraging their technical capabilities and massive user bases as they move into cultural domains. Exploiting the technical affordance of interactivity, they have been building out their own content platforms, deploying the "sharing" culture to vertically integrate services, from creating content and tools to access and control over content. The "sharing" culture was one of the celebrated characteristics of Web 2.0 which emphasized user-generated content, interactivity, and participatory culture. Initially, the Web 2.0-enabled sharing culture was seen as the democratization of the Internet; however, rather than expanding democracy, it has been quickly exploited by capital both in China and other parts of the world.[4]

The search engine was not always associated with "sharing" culture as it was initially pointing to and directing users to third-party content; however, it is no longer just linking to existing third-party information. Rather, search engine companies are vertically integrated and competing to control and produce content and create platforms where they can distribute their own content. As noted earlier, Baidu is more than providing a search function; rather it has a range of online platforms that create content which feeds into its overarching ads business. One of the most prominent of Baidu's properties is its online encyclopedia. In Chinese, encyclopedia is called *Baike* which means "hundred subjects." Compared to the traditional encyclopedia, *Baidu Baike* offers a broader range of information including food recipes, information on films, video games, etc. to draw in as many users as possible into the platform. It's little known in the US, but Baidu Baike is one of the most visited web sites in China and has over 16 million entries written by more than 6.9 million users as of October 2019.[5] Baidu Baike is often equated with the US Wikipedia because it relies on open-source software and volunteer contributors for content production. Wikipedia is often held up as an exemplar of Web 2.0 collective endeavor to show how the Internet provides a possibility to challenge market logics. However, Baidu Baike is commercially-driven and inscribed with market logics, whereas Wikipedia is a non-profit organization based on a donation-based revenue model. In Baidu Baike, user-created content is incorporated into Baidu's ads business. Whereas Wikipedia is under a Creative Commons Attribution-ShareAlike license which assures that all content is open and shareable, Baidu Baike's site displays ©2022 Baidu which means that the content belongs to Baidu. Far from a "sharing" culture that operates outside of market logic, content contributors in Baidu Baike need to relinquish their rights to Baidu with submission or editing of entries and the contributed content is locked within the walls of Baidu.[6] Within this structure, Baidu is able to bring user content into its own profit domain.

While Wikipedia volunteers are not compensated, Baidu deploys a reward system to incentivize content creators. According to the *South China Morning Post* – owned by Baidu's competitor Alibaba – Baidu Baike has 340 core contributors who are considered the "Elite Team" and who are managed by Baidu.[7] The editors are rewarded through a so-called credit system. To draw in and incentivize volunteers, Baidu uses two forms of credit systems: one is "experience value" in which contributors are evaluated based on the level of contribution regardless of search results and the second is "wealth value" which is based on the content's search results.[8] Volunteer contributors are given "experience points" and "wealth points." Experience points allow contributors to upgrade their accounts and move up hierarchically, while wealth points can be used to redeem items from snacks to smartphones from participating merchants in Baidu's mall.[9] This is a form of unfair trade or stealing as Baidu offers to "redeem items" in exchange for volunteers' intellectual output since its reward system costs much less than actually committing to salaries for workers. This labor practice is also used by Baidu Baike's long-time competitors.

With the entry of Baidu's new rival ByteDance, the competition over "sharing" culture has been renewed and intensified. Recently ByteDance launched a new search portal after acquiring a major stake in Baidu's competitor *Baike.com*, the second largest Baike behind Baidu Baike. Baike.com was established in 2005 and has long been pitted against Baidu Baike as the two sites have similar business models deploying user-generated content and user award systems.[10] In 2010, Baike's founder Pan Haidong published an open letter and filed a complaint to the State Administration for Industry and Commerce against Baidu's monopolistic practices.[11] In response, Baidu sued Baike.com which later had to pay a fine for defamation. These ongoing tensions are indicative of the fight over user-created content exploiting the "sharing culture."

Besides Baidu Baike, the company has expanded with several other content publishing platforms including Baidu's online social forum *Baidu Tieba/Baidu Post Bar*, one of the earlier social marketing platforms. Baidu Tieba, launched in 2003, allows users to create topics of interest and discuss various social issues. Baidu Tieba often is compared to social news forum *Reddit* and is similar to a bulletin board. It classifies users into groups organized under different themed "bars" or forums where users can join in and participate in discussion and search for topics of interest including food, politics, films, etc. Baidu Tieba uses the same incentive mechanism as Baidu Baike, rewarding perks to contributors. The platform not only provides user-generated content but more importantly offers information on individuals' interests and traits which are critical for Baidu's ads business. *Baidu Tieba* has almost 45 million monthly active app users.[12]

Along with *Baidu Tieba*, Baidu has a platform called *Baijiahao* which was built in response to ByteDance's news aggregator *Jinri Toutiao* and Tencent Holdings' *WeChat*. Baijiahao is a blog-like publisher platform where bloggers, writers, and journalists can publish their work in various formats. The published content on Baijiahao is directed to Baidu's newsfeed and incorporated into search results for Baidu's marketing business. As of the first quarter of 2021, Baijiahao had 4.2 million publisher accounts.[13] This is valuable for Baidu's advertising business with the amount of content created and the number of users to draw clicks.[14] Since Baidu isn't able to access content from the super-app walled gardens like WeChat, content generated from its own platforms is increasingly important.

Baidu's ads business heavily relies on a range of platforms that generate user-generated content. Baidu describes them as "community products;" they are built specifically to exploit the culture of sharing and introduce market logic into users' collective knowledge in exchange for the use of the technical platform and the dissemination of information.

Cultural Institutions

Considering that its search function hinges on fresh content, Baidu has been aggressively amassing new content to draw in ever more user traffic. To that end, Baidu launched *Baidu Encyclopedia Digital Museum* (BEDM) in 2012 with six national museums including the National Museum of China. This move was done specifically to expand the content on the Baidu Baike platform. Baidu emphasizes the non-profit side of this venture and purports that their entry into cultural institutions is meant to provide access to culture and knowledge; however, the company failed to mention that the digitization of culture is built on Baidu's private digital property platform using proprietary technologies. Baidu has experimented with myriads of new technologies – AI-aided exhibitions, cloud, augmented reality, image recognition, etc. – as the company cultivates new spaces for accumulation and proprietary technologies.

Backed by the Chinese state cultural policy which encourages the development of the cultural industry as a growth sector, in 2017, Baidu collaborated with the State Administration of Cultural Heritage to create over 2,000 digital museums.[15] The company offers virtual tours of museums including Emperor Qin Shi Huang's Mausoleum Site Museum where Baidu wraps 2,000-year-old Terracotta Warriors with cutting edge digital technologies to recreate a virtual cultural experience through Baidu's proprietary Apps.[16] Baidu Baike has expanded the scope of its culture for profit-making business by digitizing intangible folk songs and natural sounds under its Museum of Original Sound as part of its BEDM initiative.[17] Baidu's digitization of museums is commonly described as increasing China's "soft power" and cultural nationalism,[18] but museums within the cultural heritage sector are being reconfigured into profit sites for the rapidly growing economic sector.[19] Deploying its advanced technologies, Baidu has taken to pillaging cultural institutions as it is looking for long-term profitable returns by experimenting with its various proprietary technologies on cultural spaces to expand its footprint.

Baidu's search business has long struggled to carve out market space outside of China, but the company's cultural project is still trying to reach beyond its territorial boundaries. As cultural institutions around the world seek to draw more tourists and search for new revenue sources, Chinese tourists – who spent $277 billion overseas in 2018, accounting for almost one-fifth of global tourism spending – are a vital demographic target.[20] Baidu Baike teamed up with Spanish cities and tourist sites to build digital museums. Its first museum project outside of China was the Gaudí museum in Spain which presented applications of AI, virtual reality, 360-degree imaging, and audio. According to Baidu Baike, the company has extended its partnership connections with over 1,600 museums around the world including in Mexico, Germany, and Austria.[21]

Baidu's venture into cultural institutions is not without its rivals. Baidu is competing against global capital which is devouring cultural institutions at a rapid rate. Baidu's rival Tencent is also working with domestic and international museums. In 2019, Tencent embarked on its own cultural digitization project with the Palace Museum in Beijing – known as the Forbidden City – digitizing 100,000 artifacts housed in the museum.[22] Like Baidu, the company uses its own proprietary AI technology and cloud infrastructure to set technical and digital management standards for Chinese museums. Globally, Tencent signed a deal with the Guimet Museum in Paris, France – one of the largest collections of Asian art outside of Asia – to digitize the museum's collection and curate its digital exhibitions.[23] To further its cultural business, during the height of the pandemic, Tencent launched a project called "Museum in the Cloud" teaming up with 11 major US Museums including the New York Museum of Modern Art (MoMA), Asian Art Museum of San Francisco, Autry Museum of the American West, Guggenheim, etc. to reach Chinese outbound travelers.[24] The company deploys its WeChat Channels and Mini Program powered by AI which offers users a range of functions including audio tours, video materials, interactive games, and maps.[25]

Meanwhile, from a different direction, Alibaba has teamed up with the British Museum, the UK's largest cultural institution,[26] and the Metropolitan Museum of Art (MoMa) in New York selling museum branded merchandise in its e-commercial sites Tmall and Taobao.[27] Alibaba's online travel platform Fliggy has collaborated with the British Museum to livestream inside the museum guided by Chinese-speaking guides to bring back Chinese visitors.[28] Alibaba has leveraged the fact that UK cultural institutions are struggling with public funding cuts and heavily relying on corporate sponsorships to open up new lucrative Chinese markets while benefiting from drawing in more traffic. Besides Baidu's domestic rivals, Baidu is also competing globally against Google which has established *Google Arts & Culture* (GA&C) to engulf culture around the world through the digitization of books and art. GA&C is working with over 25,000 museums around the world and has already digitized more than 25 million books from libraries in many countries.[29]

In 2017, as Google began worked with Chinese publishers to add Chinese books to Google book search, Baidu soon after launched the document-sharing platform *Baidu Wenku* (Baidu Knows). Similar to DropBox or Scribd, *Baidu Wenku* allows users to upload and share documents including literary works. Baidu's incursion into the literary realm faced fierce opposition. A group of domestic best-selling authors in China and the Recording Works Committee of the China Audio-Video Association challenged both Baidu and Google for facilitating copyright infringement of literary works.[30] As discussed in an earlier chapter, Baidu was already in deep water around copyright infringement of its MP3 search services. The literature dispute led Baidu to remove 2.8 million literary works; the company was also ordered by Beijing's Haidian district court to compensate three authors.[31] On the one hand, this was a favored verdict since Baidu needed to pay only three authors $22,939 each; on the other hand, the company had to change its business model. To mitigate its copyright issues, Baidu launched its *Wenku Copyright Collaboration Platform* in 2009, where Baidu would offer commissions for sales and advertising to writers and copyright holders.[32] The company now generates revenue by providing snippets of content for free but charges a fee for full access and shares advertising revenues with copyright holders.

As Baidu has expanded its business into cultural domains, the company has shifted its earlier position of skirting copyright to now using copyright as an instrument of its capital accumulation as it has moved into the video streaming market.

Streaming Culture

Along with commodifying and commercializing the "sharing" culture and cultural institutions, Baidu has a growing footprint in the entertainment sector as they have joined the growing video streaming market – which has surpassed the number of traditional TV network viewers. China's entertainment and media market was worth $359 billion in 2021 and is expected to have an annual growth rate of 5% through 2025 to surpass $436 billion in market value.[33] The majority of that market growth is expected to be contributed by over-the-top (OTT) – aka streaming – videos, online advertising, and virtual reality sectors.[34]

In 2010, Baidu created its subsidiary *iQiyi* which is one of the largest streaming video platforms in China and often described as China's Netflix. Initially, iQiyi was a start-up backed by Providence Equity Partners. Baidu later acquired *iQiyi* which was the first Chinese video streaming site to go public in the US, issuing its IPO on the Nasdaq in 2018. Goldman Sachs (Asia) LLC, Credit Suisse BofA, and Merrill Lynch were the lead underwriters for the IPO. The company as of 2022 has 217 institutional shareholders including Goldman Sachs, Morgan Stanley, Blackrock, Bank of America, CitiGroup and Vanguard Group Inc.

Baidu owns 53% of iQiyi and holds more than 90% of the company's voting rights.[35] iQiyi generates over 30% of Baidu's total revenue but its long-term growth has been uncertain with intensifying competition in the streaming sector.[36] iQiyi's 2021 annual revenue was over 30 billion yuan, and its revenue source is different from US counterpart Netflix in that it does not rely solely on a subscription model. Instead, iQiyi has four different revenue sources: member subscriptions, online advertising, content distribution, and 'other' – for example, licensing fees. In 2021, iQiyi generated more than half of its revenue from its paid subscriptions, 25% from ads, and the rest from other businesses – including content licensing fees.[37] iQiyi offers limited free content with advertising, but subscriptions are required for full access. iQiyi represents a new business model that mixes social media, entertainment, e-commerce, and online literature.[38] In 2013, iQiyi also acquired online literature platform *Zongheng* which hosts the work of freelance writers and entered into the online literature market, competing against Tencent and Alibaba. Taken in tandem, Baidu's literature platform is used to attract original content writers. The platform is able to vertically integrate the entire lifecycle from the creation of a book to production and distribution of original TV drama and film content.

Compared to Baidu's earlier music strategy search which drew in traffic by exploiting gray areas in China's copyright law, with iQiyi, Baidu has taken the opposite approach. When initially launched, iQiyi positioned itself as a site of high-quality copyrighted content and against pirated content as China's first copyrighted video library offering movies, TV, dramas, and other content. In the mid-2000s, when Chinese video streaming began to emerge, it was driven by user-driven content overlaid with advertising models. However, the industry struggled to monetize the content because advertisers were reluctant to spend ads dollars on potentially pirated content.[39] Luzhou Li explicates that with the pressure to generate profit, the industry has had to shift from user-generated content to copyrighted content, licensing from domestic- as well as foreign content providers.[40] The PRC has assisted the industry and supported its international expansion by stepping in to tighten its copyright regime to promote its cultural industry.[41]

With this as backdrop, iQiyi was intended to appeal to advertisers and consumers as a provider of "premium quality content." iQiyi's streaming collection includes a combination of licensed- and original content. The company has stocked up domestic- as well as overseas streaming rights and invested in the production of original content featuring domestic and foreign TV series, and independent films from the US, the UK, and South Korea. The country's fast-growing streaming video industry has been opened up for Western media content providers as well as regional players such as from South Korea and Taiwan. However, in 2015 the state quickly intervened and restricted the distribution of foreign content to no more than 30% of a streaming platform.[42] While Western media often reported that the regulation was an obvious attempt by the CCP to embed ideological control,[43] the policy was more of an industrial policy to foster and provide space for the domestic traditional cultural sector over new digital platforms. Initially online distribution platforms were exempted from regulatory restrictions from showing foreign content which allowed them to quickly expand, while also challenging traditional state-sponsored broadcasters and film distributors.[44]

In China, Baidu's iQiyi and its competitors Tencent Video and Alibaba's *Youku* occupy over 80% of the market share as many US streaming companies including Netflix haven't been able to crack open the Chinese market. However, the competition is still stiff because in addition to its direct rivals Alibaba and Tencent, Baidu is competing against a range of streaming platforms encompassing the short video, live-streaming, gaming-related, and user-generated end of the spectrum – companies such as Kuaishou, Bilibili, ByteDance's Douyin (TikTok overseas), Huya, and DouYu. As newcomers are chipping away at advertising dollars from the long format streaming platforms, the copyright issue has reignited over attempts to control the streaming market.

Kuaishou, Bilibili, and Douyin have spawned a significant amount of user-generated content which often appropriates clips from TV shows and films. In response, Baidu, Alibaba, Tencent, and 70 other TV and film production companies have banded together to demand the termination of those practices.[45] Soon after, China's National Copyright Administration affirmed that they would heighten and expand their investigation into copyright infringement on short video platforms.

Ironically, in 2018, Baidu was first sued by ByteDance for copyright infringement. The lawsuit was brought against Baidu's lesser-known Huopai short video platform after someone posted content from a TikTok user on their site without permission. Baidu argued that the short video didn't constitute copyright infringement because uploaded TikTok content was too short. In 2018, the Beijing court rejected TikTok's claim because Baidu removed the content in a timely matter. However, the court ruled the first time that short videos are protected IP cementing copyright protection for short video–sharing platforms. Recently, Tencent Video also sued ByteDance for copyright violation for TikTok users uploading clips from its TV series *Crime Crackdown*;[46] meanwhile ByteDance has filed a counter-complaint against Tencent for monopolistic behavior as Tencent prohibits the sharing of Douyin content on Tencent's social media platform WeChat.[47] As the competition is heating up, the streaming companies are trying to resort to fierce copyright protection and lawsuits.[48] The contention is not just among streaming companies; rather, iQiyi is competing over consumer time and eyeballs against all content platforms such as short-form content, e-gaming, and social media.[49]

The fight over copyright illustrates that one of the main choke points for streaming companies is content. Thus, beyond being merely a conduit of third-party content, iQiyi has moved into the entertainment industry, producing various original content ranging from drama series, films, animation, and variety shows in order to draw in new subscribers and advertisers. iQiyi is not the only one betting on original content. Its competitors Alibaba and Tencent are investing millions of dollars in content production.[50]

As the domestic market continues to heat up, iQiyi has been looking to find new streaming markets beyond China. While iQiyi's "going out" is seen as a response to CCP's cultural policy to expand the influence of Chinese culture around the world, the market imperative has spurred Baidu to seek new markets outside China. To reach global markets, iQiyi's strategies are deeply integrated into global media markets.

iQiyi has pursued strategies of co-production, content localization, and corporate partnerships with local companies outside China.[51] iQiyi first attempted to enter the Taiwanese market – a logical choice since Taiwan is the second-biggest Chinese-speaking market outside China. However, as Elaine Jing Zhao noted, the mainland Chinese companies face more rigid rules in Taiwan.[52] In 2016, iQiyi planned to establish a local subsidiary for its streaming service; however, its application was denied because Chinese investment in broadcasting entertainment content in Taiwan is prohibited under the Taiwanese *Act Governing Relations Between the People of the Taiwan Area and the Mainland Area* also called the Cross-Strait Act.

To get around the Cross-Strait Act, iQiyi used its Hong Kong subsidiary to form a partnership with a Taiwanese streaming service provider which worked with Taiwanese talent, movie directors, and producers to create original content.[53] Baidu's international expansion continued to face the harsh realities of geopolitical tensions and regulatory uncertainty making the ground unstable under iQiyi's global market expansion strategy.

Joining the US in taking a strong policy stance toward Chinese tech companies, in 2020 Taiwan's National Communications Commission (NCC) passed a draft bill regulating Internet services including foreign streaming media service providers and proposed to make it illegal for Taiwan's telecom and Internet service providers to work with any Chinese content companies.[54] Thus, iQiyi – along with Tencent who was also operating in Taiwan – was banned from operating in Taiwan.[55] As access to its largest international market was blocked, iQiyi has aggressively targeted other streaming markets in Southeast Asia. This region has become the newest battleground for streaming platforms. In 2020, Disney launched in Indonesia and Singapore, Netflix has ramped up its operations in the region, and Tencent's WeTV acquired Malaysian streaming platform Iflix.[56] iQiyi is aiming to position itself to be a regional streaming platform and so is targeting Thailand, Malaysia, Indonesia, the Philippines, and Singapore, the fastest-growing markets in the region.

As the company sets its sights on the global market, iQiyi has bet on its diverse collection of content that includes soap operas, animation, documentaries, and original programs. It continues to expand its collection, joining the content war between the various Chinese and US services. In 2018, iQiyi spent $3.2 billion on content creation which was close to the total spent on content creation by China's top six broadcaster groups put together.[57] To beef up its content library, iQiyi has also been co-producing local content in local languages to appeal to regional markets as well as licensing foreign content. In 2017, iQiyi had an exclusive agreement with

Warner Bros to license 200 films.[58] This was followed by iQiyi's licensing agreement with 20th Century Fox, NBC Universal, Paramount, and Lionsgate.[59] iQiyi is looking to enhance its global appeal while US companies are trying to use iQiyi to gain better access into the Chinese market.

iQiyi is also heavily invested in South Korean drama production, one of the most popular content in China and across the southeast Asian market. The company co-produces original content with and has exclusive licenses for more content from major South Korean studios such as CJ Entertainment, SBS, JTBC Studio, etc.[60] However, these strategic partnerships have been constrained by geopolitical tensions after a joint decision by South Korea and the US to deploy the US Terminal High Altitude Area Defense (THAAD) anti-missile system to the southeastern region of the Korean Peninsula and deepen bilateral defense cooperation – which drew protests from peace activists and residents against U.S. militarization in the region.[61]

Beijing saw this move as Washington's attempt at containment of China and in response put restrictions on South Korean cultural goods and entertainment exports to mainland China,[62] though iQiyi's international arm continued to stream new Korean content to markets outside China. After six years, China signaled that it would lift the restrictions which allowed iQiyi to once again offer new Korean dramas in mainland China.[63]

iQiyi has tapped into the popularity of the "K-wave" to compete and reach regional markets considering that South Korean content is even more consumed than US content on streaming platforms in major key South Asian Markets – especially in Thailand, Indonesia, Singapore, and the Philippines.[64] However, the benefit is not just one way. iQiyi also offers South Korean media companies an avenue to reach both the Chinese market and the regional Asian markets. For instance, the mutual cooperation agreement between iQiyi and Korean entertainment giant CJ is not only about co-producing original content, but the two also reached an agreement to make CJ's content available via stream on the iQiyi platform in Singapore, Malaysia, Indonesia, Thailand, Philippines, and Vietnam.[65] In that same vein, iQiyi has joined with the Philippines' major media company ABS-CBN to produce original Filipino dramas exclusively on the iQiyi platform. In 2020, iQiyi announced it would establish local offices in Thailand, Malaysia, the Philippines, and Indonesia and build local labor forces in South Korea and Japan. iQiyi also launched its service in March 2021 across the

UAE, Saudi Arabia, and Egypt, targeting three of the largest markets in the middle East and North Africa (MENA) region. Additionally, the company rolled out a Spanish language streaming service targeting Latin America.

Even with all this global expansion into developing markets, iQiyi is still struggling to gain new subscribers both domestically and internationally as the company is spending millions on content acquisition to compete against the other global media behemoths. In December 2021, the *Financial Times* reported that the top eight US media companies planned to spend at least $115 billion to secure new movies and television shows for their video streaming platforms.[66] This forced Baidu's hand, and at the end of 2021, the company laid off more than 20% of its staff and raised subscription prices as both cost-cutting and capital-raising measures to prop up its depressed stock value.[67] The *NY Times* reported that Baidu's layoff was due to the PRC's crackdown which was hurting tech companies.[68] However, despite its dominant presence in the Chinese streaming market, like many other streaming companies, iQiyi has never been profitable because of the capital-intensive nature of its business. iQiyi's subscriptions dropped from over 100 million to 97 million during the peak of the Covid pandemic when people were spending hours online and subscribing to multiple streaming services.[69] With ferocious competition and rising costs of production and acquisition of content, even Netflix, which was considered the only game in the town for streaming, suffered losses of 200,000 subscribers in the first three months of 2022 and its shares plunged. Subsequently, Warner Bros. Discovery shut down its CNN+ streaming service after two weeks. There will be increasing concentration in the streaming market as the competition heats up. iQiyi's survival in global markets against the deep-pocketed players like Apple, Amazon, Disney, etc. is uncertain.

For iQiyi, fierce competition is not the only problem. As of this writing, iQiyi along with its parent company Baidu was among five companies the US Securities and Exchange Commission (SEC) added to the list of companies which may face delisting from the US stock market under the Holding Foreign Companies Accountability Act (HFCAA).[70] Facing unprecedented challenges – geopolitical pressure in the global market, cutthroat domestic and international competition, and rising content costs – Baidu's iQiyi has had to inject global capital, raising $285 million from its shareholders and private investors in order to sustain itself; however, whether and how iQiyi is able to reboot its growth remains in question.

Conclusion

This chapter examines Baidu's cultural profile, showing how the company is trying to augment its profit domains. The company has introduced market logics and expanded its property relations by navigating copyrights to cultural domains from multiple directions. Baidu has exploited the "sharing culture" by appropriating user-generated content and volunteer unwaged labor for its search advertising business. Meanwhile, the company is also digitizing and commodifying cultural institutions which hadn't yet been fully absorbed into the marketplace. The company is collaborating with Chinese cultural institutions and overseas partners to digitize public museums and transform them into its profit-making sites. Baidu's incursion into the cultural domain was also driven by the company's domestic and global competitors Alibaba, Tencent, and Google. In fact, the expansion of the cultural industry and increasing competition over culture have accompanied the strengthening of China's copyright regime.

With an ascending role for copyright/licensing and ravenous and growing Internet consumption, Baidu has moved into the adjacent bourgeoning streaming market. To appeal to a wider audience, Baidu has strategically diversified its service through the production of local content and partnerships with foreign content providers. Baidu being a part of the global cultural industry has become a major provider for Korean, Netflix, and Hollywood content. Baidu's cultural business illustrates how culture has turned into a trillion-dollar industry to become a new economic engine.

In the 14th Five Year Plan (FYP), the PRC has set out a plan to accelerate the digitization of the cultural industry – digital publishing, digital entertainment, online streaming, films, TV dramas, Games, etc. – and encourage companies to "go global." The party state also stated that it was "putting social benefits first and uniting social and economic benefits and strengthen[ing] the modern cultural industry system and market system."[71] The question remains, how will the CCP prioritize both social benefit and needs and the market system for culture?

Notes

1 See Henry Jenkins, *Convergence Culture: Where Old and New Media Collide* (New York: New York University Press, 2006), 4; Clay Shirky, *Cognitive Surplus: Creativity and Generosity in a Connected Age* (New York: Penguin, 2010), 213, 27; Axel Bruns, *Blogs, Wikipedia, Second*

Life, and beyond from Production to Produsage (New York: Peter Lang, 2008), 341.
2 Herbert Schiller, *Culture, Inc.: The Corporate Takeover of Public Expression* (New York: Oxford University Press, 1991).
3 Shi-lianShan, "Chinese Cultural Policy and the Cultural Industries," *City, Culture and Society* 5, no. 3 (2014): 115–121.
4 Matthew Hindman, *The Myth of Digital Democracy* (Princeton, NJ: Princeton University Press, 2009).
5 Jane Zhang, "How Baidu built an encyclopedia with 16 times more Chinese entries than Wikipedia," *South Morning China,* November 20, 2019, https://sg.news.yahoo.com/baidu-baike-faced-off-against-080541967.html.
6 Ibid.
7 Jane Zhang, "How Baidu built an encyclopedia with 16 times more Chinese entries than Wikipedia," *South Morning China*, November 20, 2019, https://sg.news.yahoo.com/baidu-baike-faced-off-against-080541967.html.
8 Jiangtao Wang, Jianmei Yang, Quan Chen, and Sang-Bing Tsai, "Creating the Sustainable Conditions for Knowledge Information Sharing in Virtual Community," S*pringerplus*, 5, no. 1019 (2018): 1–9.
9 Ibid.
10 Lara Farrar, "It's tricky for wikis and online encyclopedias in China," *CNN*, October 14, 2009, http://www.cnn.com/2009/TECH/10/14/wiki.china/index.html.
11 Michael Kan, "China's Baidu accused of search bias in monopoly complaint," *ComputerWorld*, February 24, 2011, https://www.computerworld.com/article/2747850/china-s-baidu-accused-of-search-bias-in-monopoly-complaint.html.
12 Lai Lin Thomala, "Monthly active users of main content sharing apps in China 2021," *Statista,* March 24, 2022, https://www.statista.com/statistics/1254262/china-leading-content-sharing-apps-monthly-active-users/.
13 Lai Lin Thomala, "Publisher number of Baidu's Baijiahao Q3 2018–Q1 2021," *Statista*, June 2, 2021, https://www-statista-com.stanford.idm.oclc.org/statistics/1080019/baidu-baijiaohao-publisher-number/.
14 Fang Kecheng, "How Baidu learned to stop worrying and love the walled garden," *Sixth Tone*, January 28, 2019, https://www.sixthtone.com/news/1003497/how-baidu-learned-to-stop-worrying-and-love-the-walled-garden.
15 Wang Kaihao, "Govt, Baidu to jointly create 2,000 online museums," *China Daily*, December 5, 2017, https://www.chinadaily.com.cn/culture/2017-12/05/content_35214898.htm.
16 Sheila Yu, "Baidu restores Terracotta Army with AR," *technode*, May 22, 2017, https://technode.com/2017/05/22/baidu-restores-terracotta-army-with-ar/.
17 "Encyclopedia of intangible cultural heritage," Baidu, https://baike.baidu.com/feiyi?lang=en.
18 Fenghua Zhang and Pascal Courty, "The China Museum Boom: Soft Power and Cultural Nationalism," *International Journal of Cultural Policy*, 27, no. 1 (2021): 30–47.

19 Emma Li, "How China has turned museum relics into big business," Vogue Business, October 1, 2021, https://www.voguebusiness.com/fashion/how-china-has-turned-museum-relics-into-big-business.
20 "Guidelines for Success in the Chinese outbound tourism market," World Tourism Organization, 2019, https://www.e-unwto.org/doi/epdf/10.18111/9789284421138.
21 Baidu, Twitter post, September 17, 2018, 8:05 a.m., https://twitter.com/baidu_inc/status/1041659281387352064.
22 Song Jingli, "Tencent teams up with Beijing's Forbidden City for digitalization and content co-production," *KrAsia*, September 17, 2019, https://kr-asia.com/tencent-teams-up-with-beijings-forbidden-city-for-digitalization-and-content-co-production.
23 Matthew Lubin, "France's Asian Art Collection Goes Digital with Tencent," *Jing Culture and Commerce*, February 4, 2019, https://jingculturecommerce.com/france-asian-art-tencent/.
24 " WeChat is Taking Museums to the Cloud," *Bloomberg*, May 1,2020, https://www.bloomberg.com/press-releases/2020-05-01/wechat-is-taking-museums-to-the-cloud.
25 Ibid.
26 Cristina Ruiz, "Museums grapple with ethics of China projects," *The Art Newspaper*, September 1, 2020, https://www.theartnewspaper.com/2020/09/01/museums-grapple-with-ethics-of-china-projects.
27 Lao Bei, "New York's Met Museum launches a flagship on Alibaba's Tmall," *KrAsia*, May 9, 2019, https://kr-asia.com/new-yorks-met-museum-launches-a-flagship-on-alibabas-tmall.
28 "Natural History Museum livestream partnership with Alibaba platform reaches new Chinese audiences," *Museums + Heritage*, January 21, 2021, https://advisor.museumsandheritage.com/news/natural-history-museum-livestream-partnership-with-alibaba-platform-reaches-new-chinese-audiences/.
29 Dan Schiller and ShinJoung Yeo, "Powered by Google: Widening access and tightening corporate control," *Red Art*. 20, no.1 (2014): 44–56.
30 Loretta Chao, "In bow to authors, Baidu scrubs document sharing site," *Wall Street Journal*, March 30, 2011, https://www.wsj.com/articles/BL-CJB-13557.
31 Ibid.
32 Wang Jing, Wuhong Yuran and Wang Shanshan, "Reluctantly, Baidu refreshes copyright stance," *Market Watch*, April 12, 2011, https://www.marketwatch.com/story/reluctantly-baidu-refreshes-copyright-stance-2011-04-12.
33 Lai Lin Thomala, "Value of the Chinese entertainment and media market 2014–2025," *Statista,* September 28, 2021.
34 Ibid.
35 "EXCLUSIVE Baidu in talks to sell majority stake in iQIYI, China's answer to Netflix -sources," *Reuters*, June 15, 2022, https://reut.rs/3NZuxL9.
36 "Baidu announces fourth quarter and Fiscal Year 2021 Results," Baidu, March 1, 2022, https://ir.baidu.com/node/13146/pdf.
37 Lai Lin Thomala, "Chinese online video platform iQiyi's annual revenue 2021, by segment," *Statista*, April 1, 2022.

38 Vinnie Lauria, "This $360 billion e-commerce trend is huge in Asia – and it's coming to the US next," *Fast Company*, October 7, 2021, https://www.fastcompany.com/90683882/social-ecommerce-asia-trend.
39 Lucy Montgomery and Eric Priest, "Copyright in China's Digital Cultural Industries'," in *Handbook of Cultural and Creative Industries in China*, ed. Michael Keane (Cheltenham: Edward Elgar Publishing, 2016), 347.
40 Luzhou Li, *Zoning China Online Video, Popular Culture, and the State* (Cambridge, MA: MIT Press, 2019), 110, 139.
41 Elaine Jing Zhao, "Negotiating State and Copyright Territorialities in Overseas Expansion: The Case of China's Online Video Streaming Platforms," *Media Industries* 5, no. 1 (2018), DOI:10.3998/mij.15031809.0005.107.
42 Lilian Lin, "China to tighten limit on foreign TV and video imports," *Wall Street Journal,* November 16, 2015, https://www.wsj.com/articles/china-to-tighten-limit-on-foreign-tv-and-video-imports-1447672849.
43 Ibid.
44 Yu Hong, *Networking China: The Digital Transformation of the Chinese Economy* (Champaign: University of Illinois Press, 2017), 106.
45 Niki Sun, "Alibaba, Baidu and Tencent learn Netflix lessons in content fight," *Financial Times*, June 5, 2021, https://www-ft-com.stanford.idm.oclc.org/content/ac4ebc50-457b-4131-99b0-669340d3389b.
46 "Tencent Video Sues Bytedance's Douyin for Copyright Infringement," *Pandaily*, August 19, 2021, https://pandaily.com/tencent-video-sues-bytedances-douyin-for-copyright-infringement/.
47 Rebeca Davis, "ByteDance files $14 million suit against Tencent for monopolistic behavior," *Variety*, February 2, 2021, https://variety.com/2021/digital/news/bytedance-douyin-tencent-lawsuit-monopoly-1234898734/.
48 Filippo Gilardi et al., "From Copycat to Copyright: Intellectual Property Amendments and the Development of Chinese Online Video Industries," *International Journal of Cultural Policy*, February 2022, DOI:10.1080/10286632.2022.2040494.
49 Karishma Hingorani, "Feature: Behind iQIYI's Niche-Driven expansion strategy," *Digital Studio*, September 12, 2021, https://www.digitalstudiome.com/production/content-business/behind-iqiyi-niche-driven-expansion-strategy.
50 "Alibaba, Baidu and Tencent learn Netflix lessons in content fight," *Nikkei Asia*, June 1, 2021, https://asia.nikkei.com/Business/Media-Entertainment/Alibaba-Baidu-and-Tencent-learn-Netflix-lessons-in-content-fight2.
51 Rebecca Davis, "China's iQIYI hires Kelvin Yau as first Thailand GM," *Variety,* January 3, 2020, https://variety.com/2020/digital/news/china-thailand-expansion-iqiyi-bbc-studios-kelvin-yau-1203455749/.
52 Zhao, "Negotiating State and Copyright Territorialities."
53 Ibid.
54 George Liao, "Taiwan passes draft bill to cut out Chinese media service providers," *Taiwan News*, July 16, 2020, https://www.taiwannews.com.tw/en/news/3968382.

55 Vivienne Chow, "Taiwan confirms ban on Chinese streaming firms iQIYI and Tencent," Variety, August 19, 2020, https://variety.com/2020/streaming/asia/taiwan-ban-china-streaming-services-iqiyi-wetv-1234739711/.
56 "China's IQIYI to Develop Regional Stars for Southeast Asia Push," *Reuters*, March 17, 2021, https://www.usnews.com/news/technology/articles/2021-03-17/chinas-iqiyi-to-develop-regional-stars-for-southeast-asia-push.
57 Eli M. Noam, *The Technology, Business, and Economics of Streaming Video the Next Generation of Media Emerges* (Northampton: Edward Elgar Publishing, 2021), 158.
58 Patrick Brzeski, "Warner Bros. Licenses 200 films to Chinese streaming giant iQiyi," *Hollywood*, March 21, 2017, https://www.hollywoodreporter.com/movies/movie-news/warner-bros-licenses-200-films-chinese-streaming-giant-iqiyi-987582/.
59 Etan Vlessing, "Lionsgate signs new movie licensing deal with China's iQiyi," *Hollywood*, November 29, 2016, https://www.hollywoodreporter.com/news/general-news/lionsgate-signs-new-movie-licensing-deal-chinas-iqiyi-950855/.
60 Patrick Frater, "IQiyi sets 'Bad and Crazy' as third Korean series for international markets," *Variety,* September 7, 2021, https://variety.com/2021/global/asia/iqiyi-bad-and-crazy-korean-series-1235057701/.
61 "U.S. Deploys Missile System Amid Rising Tensions with N. Korea," *Democracy Now*, March 8. 2017, https://www.democracynow.org/2017/3/8/headlines/us_deploys_missile_system_amid_rising_tensions_with_n_korea.
62 Matt Stiles, "Upset over a U.S. missile defense system, China hits South Korea where it hurts – in the wallet," *LA Times,* February 28. 2018, https://www.latimes.com/world/asia/la-fg-china-south-korea-tourism-20180228-htmlstory.html.
63 Patrick Frater, "Chinese streamer iQiyi seeks funding as it blocks Ukraine coverage, courts controversy over Korean drama," *Variety*, March 9, 2022, https://variety.com/2022/tv/asia/iqiyi-funding-ukraine-soccer-korea-1235199740/.
64 Patrick Frater, "Korean and US Content dominate streaming consumption in Southeast Asia," *Variety*, March 1, 2021, https://variety.com/2021/streaming/asia/korean-and-u-s-content-dominate-streaming-consumption-in-southeast-asia-1234918246/.
65 Richard Middleton, "Korea's CJENM strikes content deal with Chinese streamer iQiyi," *Television Business International*, August 5, 2020, https://tbivision.com/2020/08/05/koreas-cjenm-strikes-content-deal-with-chinese-streamer-iqiyi/.
66 Anna Nicolaou in New York and Christopher Grimes, "Streaming Wars Drive Media Groups to spend more than $100bn on new content," *Financial Times*, December 29, 2021.
67 Patrick Frater, "iQiyi cuts losses to $968 million as subscriber numbers slip," *Variety*, March 1, 2022, https://variety.com/2022/biz/news/iqiyi-cuts-losses-subscriber-numbers-1235192749/.

68 Li Yuan, "As Beijing takes control, Chinese Tech companies lose jobs and hope," *New York Times*, January 5, 2022, https://www.nytimes.com/2022/01/05/technology/china-tech-internet-crackdown-layoffs.html.

69 Patrick Frater, "Chinese streamer iQiyi's Woes have been long in the making," *Variety*, December 23, 2021, https://variety.com/2021/global/asia/chinese-streamer-iqiyi-woes-1235142076/.

70 Holding Foreign Companies Accountable Act ("HFCAA"), US Securities and Exchange Commission, https://www.sec.gov/hfcaa.

71 Outline of the People's Republic of China 14th Five-Year Plan for National Economic and Social Development and Long-Range Objectives for 2035, trans, *Xinhua News Agency*, March 12, 2021, https://cset.georgetown.edu/wp-content/uploads/t0284_14th_Five_Year_Plan_EN.pdf.

Conclusion

The study of the Chinese-based search giant Baidu illustrates the dynamics of China's Internet sectors which have become deeply integrated into and entwined with the US-led global capitalist system. The history and arc of Baidu's development show that the ascendence of China's Internet industry was a result of the party state that enabled it to create conditions for the growth of its domestic Internet sector through building out necessary network and legal infrastructures, managing the terms and flow of transnational capital and integrating into global capitalist markets. Baidu arose as a dominant search platform in the era of accelerated economic coupling between China and the US-led capitalist system centered around the Internet sector. The decades of this "coupling" have brought the interdependence of technologies, politics, and economies between the two global power states. However, China's rapid development and expansion of its domestic high-tech Internet sector which is a linchpin of current capitalism has raised fears in the US over its global hegemonic position and the inter-state rivalry today.

With the dotcom boom in the late 1990s, Baidu was one of many Chinese tech companies that tapped into transnational capital and debuted on the US stock exchange. The company used the corporate VIE (variable interest entity) structure, a work-around commonly used by China's Internet companies to draw in foreign capital by circumventing restrictions on foreign direct investment in the value-added Internet services with the Chinese and US governments' tacit backing for their mutual interest. The development of Baidu – and other Chinese tech giants – exposes the limitation of the state-centered "US vs China" analysis considering the extent of entanglement of Chinese and the US capital over the Internet.

Transnational capital has long backed China's search market – facilitated by the Chinese state – and quickly turned it into a highly

DOI: 10.4324/9781003189893-6

dynamic and competitive market. Early on, Baidu had to compete against other domestic private and state search companies – Qihoo, Sogou, Soso, Jike, and Panguso – as well as the US search engines Google, Yahoo!, and Bing. Initially, Baidu was able to gain a large share of the search market in China by exploiting, maneuvering, and shaping China's evolving copyright regulatory regime, leveraging local linguistic and other advantages, and building strategic partnerships with domestic and foreign capital. Baidu's dominant search position in China has most often seen as being due to the People's Republic of China (PRC)'s backing and Google's partial exit from mainland China in 2010. However, this explanation conceals the fact that transnational capital has long fueled China's burgeoning Internet sector.

Within China's booming domestic Internet market, Baidu's position has been far from secure since its early years as a number of Baidu's counterparts quickly joined the race to marketize the Internet. Alibaba, Tencent, JD.com, ByteDance, and Meituan have all competed fiercely over Baidu's main revenue source of digital advertising. Worse, with the emergence of walled-garden super apps like Tencent's WeChat and Alibaba's Taobao as well as the growth of the mobile space, Baidu's search function, which relies on indexing the public web, has stymied the growth of Baidu's user base. Domestic inter-capitalist competition has necessitated that Baidu search for new domestic sectors and international markets for further expansion. However, Baidu's sectoral and international expansion have been met with inter-capitalist competition and geopolitical pressures.

Baidu has struggled to move into adjacent markets like e-commerce, social media, and gaming and it has failed to expand into global markets. Baidu spent more than ten years investing millions of dollars into its international ventures; but it has been far from successful despite the company continually searching to retool its global market outreach and keep the embers glowing. After decades in internet business, Baidu's revenue is still largely limited to its domestic market. While the company has had to retreat from its mostly search-related international expansion, in the cultural sector, Baidu has been exploiting the "sharing" culture and digitizing both domestic and international cultural institutions to absorb culture into its profit site. In particular, Baidu has joined the booming streaming sector, establishing its subsidiary iQiyi, and has been trying to reach global markets and targeting strong growth regional markets in particular through localization of content, co-production and local partnerships. However, its transnationalizing efforts face ongoing geopolitical tensions and streaming wars with a flood of global players like Netflix, Disney Plus, HBO Max, Apple TV Plus, and Amazon.

Under extreme competitive pressure in both domestic and international markets, Baidu has had to locate new growth engines, and has reoriented its business toward becoming an Artificial Intelligence (AI) company. Baidu is now pushing its AI technologies as a major business under the slogan of "all in AI."[1] The company has become more than a search engine company as it has constructed a range of new growth sectors built on AI – AVs, EVs, IoT, AI cloud, AI chips, health, and fintech. As demonstrated throughout the book, in order for Baidu's new AI businesses to continue to grow, it is just not sufficient to rely on its technological capabilities for an ongoing competitive edge; rather, Baidu has preemptively secured thousands of AI patents with which to control AI sectors and has pursued strategic partnerships with both domestic and foreign companies. Far from decoupling, AVs, one of Baidu's core AI businesses, is also built on a series of foreign partnerships extending its global alliance from car manufacturers to chip makers to insurance services. More importantly, Baidu is relying on the PRC's new economic policy that pivots from the consumer-oriented internet to the industrial internet; at the same time the company is navigating between domestic policy and the geopolitical rivalry between the US and China.

Hedging against the current geopolitical turmoil, the Chinese party state is accelerating its economic restructuring from the workshop of the world to produce high value capital intensive goods, and seeking to alleviate its reliance on foreign-controlled core technologies, bolster global supply chains, and boost next-generation Internet technologies and embed them into the industrial sectors embodied by AI, 5G, data, cloud, blockchain, IoT, etc. To pursue this new phase of Chinese economic transformation, the party state has deployed a multifaceted approach – trying to shore up political power over its tech sectors by drawing in the large and dynamic private tech companies into its economic plans, creating new regulatory regimes, incentivizing them with tax subsidies, creating a business-friendly environment for growth markets, and financing R&D. Baidu is not outside the party state's new economic projects that have been powered by nearly $1 trillion in government funding.

Baidu is designated as one of the "national AI champions" – along with Alibaba and Tencent – that is participating in China's AI-driven infrastructure, a key economic engine, and has become allied with the CCP's industrial policy as a corporate strategy. The company has begun to aggressively pursue working with local governments and industrial sectors and has become involved in the building of new local and national infrastructures. On the surface and from across the Pacific, this could be seen as Baidu and the private Internet companies and sectors being managed by Chinese state policy. However, leveraging its AI technology, capital, technical infrastructure, talent, and R&D facilities for a competitive edge, Baidu has long been sitting at the center of China's political circles and the government-academic-industrial complex and has made the competitive decision to capitalize on China's new economic development that emphasizes technological innovation.

The Chinese government's recent crackdown on the oversized private tech sector with antitrust cases and new data regulations has been seen as a clash between the Chinese state and its private Internet giants. However, the case of Baidu illustrates that the reality is more complicated. Indeed, the CCP's new measures have jolted China's Internet sector, wiping away hundreds of billions from the market, and has signaled the CCP's renewed market intervention. The CCP's purpose of these new measures is not one dimensional though. The CCP is aiming to reassert its power over the most dynamic economic sector – the Internet – as the state pursues structural reforms. However, this doesn't mean that the PRC intends to seize control over the private Internet sector and certainly isn't aiming to block foreign capital.

Rather, for its legitimacy, the party state has responded to the domestic and global political economic dynamism confronting the mounting challenges – the ongoing trade war, rising income and regional inequality, export-driven growth, falling growth rate, etc. To combat these social and structural problems, the CCP is in the midst of setting a new stage for the next generation digital economy that it hopes will move beyond the low-wage form of production and put China in a better position within a global capitalist market. However, China's political economic restructuring process will not happen without coordination, clashes, and contradictions of the interests of different units of capital and various social and political forces including the proposed "people-centered" development of the 14th Five Year Plan (FYP) and president Xi's "common prosperity" campaign in which he has promised to redistribute wealth and prioritize social needs over market- and economic growth. Within this new political economic environment, Baidu is retuning its corporate strategies not to reorient its business for social needs but in order to capture much-needed capital accumulation opportunities for the company's continuing profit maximization and survival.

Note

1 Kelsey Cheng, "At the right place, at the right time: How Baidu is cementing its position as a leading AI Company," *Pandaily*, March 23, 2021, https://pandaily.com/at-the-right-place-at-the-right-time-how-baidu-is-cementing-its-position-as-a-leading-ai-company/.

Index

For Product Safety Concerns and Information please contact our EU representative GPSR@taylorandfrancis.com Taylor & Francis Verlag GmbH, Kaufingerstraße 24, 80331 München, Germany

Printed and bound by CPI Group (UK) Ltd, Croydon, CR0 4YY
14/09/2026
02216243-0006